GROUP TECHNIQUES FOR IDEA BUILDING

Second Edition

Applied Social Research Methods Series
Volume 9

APPLIED SOCIAL RESEARCH
METHODS SERIES

Series Editors:
LEONARD BICKMAN, Peabody College, Vanderbilt University, Nashville
DEBRA J. ROG, Vanderbilt University, Washington, DC

GROUP TECHNIQUES FOR IDEA BUILDING

Second Edition

Carl M. Moore

Applied Social Research Methods Series
Volume 9

SAGE Publications
International Educational and Professional Publisher
Thousand Oaks   London   New Delhi

For information address:

 SAGE Publications, Inc.
2455 Teller Road
Thousand Oaks, California 91320

SAGE Publications Ltd.
6 Bonhill Street
London EC2A 4PU
United Kingdom

SAGE Publications India Pvt. Ltd.
M-32 Market
Greater Kailash I
New Delhi 110 048 India

Printed in the United States of America

Library of Congress Cataloging-in-Publication Data

Moore, Carl M.
    Group techniques for idea building / Carl M. Moore.—2nd ed.
        p.   cm.—(Applied social research methods series; v. 9)
    Includes bibliographical references.
    ISBN 0-8039-5642-8 (cl).—ISBN 0-8039-5643-6 (pb)
    1. Group problem solving. 2. Decision making, Group. 3. Social
groups. I. Title. II. Series.
HM131.M615   1994
302.3—dc20   93-44777

94 95 96 97 98   10 9 8 7 6 5 4 3 2 1

Sage Production Editor: Rebecca Holland

Contents

Preface to the Second Edition

This book retains the goal of the first edition, to provide clear, complete, useful descriptions of selected task-oriented processes that the reader can use to help groups of people generate, develop, and select among ideas. The processes are used to enable small groups to address a specific planning or decision-making task, and are often used in combination.

CHANGES IN THE SECOND EDITION

This book appears in a series on Applied Social Research, "designed to provide students and practicing professionals in the social sciences with . . . textbooks describing the major methods used in applied social research." The response to the first edition—who purchased the book and how they made use of it—indicates that it has achieved that end. But my goal is for the book to be useful to a broad spectrum of people exasperated by problems that bedevil groups, who need tools to help groups be more productive. My greatest satisfaction from the first edition came from readers who were looking for processes to enhance the productivity of groups.

Consider, for example, two people who conduct applied social research but are interested in the potential of the processes to enhance group productivity.

- Jin Hui Ong, previous Director of the Center for Advanced Studies at the National University of Singapore and current chair of the department of sociology, won a Fulbright to come to the United States to work with me. He wished to determine whether the processes might work in his culture as leaders begin to include more people in making decisions about their society.
- Brad Parks, a researcher with the United States Department of Energy, assembled a large group of people representing different agencies and different research traditions. He was interested in how together they might increase utilization of a new kind of geophysical mapping. He was interested

in how the processes might be adapted, not to do research but to have a successful meeting.

Many people who direct community leadership programs have found the processes especially suitable. The programs identify diverse groups of leaders in their communities (usually between 25 and 50) and then have them meet for a full day once a month (usually for about 9 months).

> The explicit goals of such programs are to identify and nurture existing and potential community leaders, to increase their knowledge of the community, and to develop networks of individuals who can help each other solve community problems. Underlying these goals is the assumption that increased knowledge of the community, coupled with a network of affiliations, will enable the graduates to be more effective participants in the civic life of the community. (Moore, 1991)

Community leadership programs adopted *Group Techniques for Idea Building* to introduce tools that program participants could use with groups composed of people from diverse parts of the community, not because they expected them to conduct applied social research.

The processes described here have considerable utility for potential and practicing applied social researchers. However, people with pragmatic concerns about the productivity of groups can and should use them, without any thought about "research."

Readers familiar with *Group Techniques for Idea Building* will recognize modifications, additions, and deletions to the first edition. Some chapters have been eliminated and, although all chapters have been at least partly rewritten, there are three major revisions.

The chapter on Interpretive Structural Modeling (ISM) presents a much "friendlier" way to use the process, without depending on a computer to store the choices that the group makes. ISM is a very powerful tool, primarily because it provides an effective way to help groups do what they most strongly resist—make choices. The most feedback I received about the first edition was about ISM, principally because earlier descriptions of ISM appeared only in the engineering professional literature where all versions of it required use of a mainframe computer. The new chapter makes ISM more generally accessible.

Following each of the chapters that describe the three processes are step-by-step, detailed descriptions of exactly what someone might say and do when using each of the processes. These sections have been written from the perspective of the reader as facilitator. They come as close as I am able, in print, to replicate what I say and do when using them. My hope is that they integrate all of the elements in a way that will overcome apprehensions and motivate people to try them. The chapter on the Delphi Technique in the first edition has been eliminated. Although I have used Delphi extensively and it is an effective group process, particularly when members of a group cannot or should not meet face-to-face, I do not believe I have found a way to explicate the Delphi Technique that improves on descriptions in other sources. Moreover, the bulk of the chapter—strategies to improve responses to mail questionnaires—did not make a unique contribution to the literature on survey research methods. Paradoxically, in our ever-shrinking world, tools that enable us to work together across space and time are vitally important. I urge the reader to look for them elsewhere, because this book focuses on a few useful ways to help people meet face to face.

The first edition's use of the word *technique* has been replaced with this edition's use of *process*. It is not a big change; sometimes people use the two terms interchangeably. *Process* has a more desirable connotation. *Technique* is associated on one hand with tactical manipulation and on the other with artistry or skill. I do not want to appear naive; any method, approach, technique, or process can be used for good or ill. However, I prefer the connotations of procedure or modus operandi, two common understandings of process. I want to avoid the suggestion that the group processes described in this book require substantial skill or artistry.

Two colleagues and friends, Ken Parker and Jack Gargan, coauthored the original chapter on ISM. I have modified it substantially, particularly with the instructions on how to conduct ISM without a computer, so it is unfair to them to include their names on this edition. I am indebted to them for their insights on how to explain such a complex process.

Several people assisted in the evolution of my thinking about these processes and helped with the preparation of this edition. Special thanks go to Claude Malone, administrator without peer, a leader willing to serve his community by taking the chances necessary to risk success. A number of the stories can be told because Claude had problems to solve and was open to administrative approaches to solve them. This edition has been improved in a variety of ways because of suggestions by Janet Ackerman, Anne Sokolowski, and David Powers.

This edition is dedicated to the quickest group process students I have ever known, the newly elected mayor and four council members of

Kamenice, Czechoslovakia. Three of us—I accompanied my good friends Eleanor Cooper and Milenko Matanovic—went there to hear their story about the velvet revolution. We learned that locally elected village leaders were asked to perform impossible jobs, without resources, traditions, or even a language for solving problems.. They understood that they needed to involve citizens in public decisions, but did not know how. It was my honor to assist the council in setting priorities. Two translators converted Czech into English and English into Czech so that we could use the Nominal Group Technique to identify what they had to do to improve their community. They recognized intuitively that the group process they had learned was a useful tool. The next day the mayor and council met with developers to talk about strategies to build a village "center." When the developers started to discuss the pros and cons of the first option offered, the mayor explained that they should get out all the options before they considered any of them in detail. The people of Kamenice face tremendous challenges, but at least their leaders can use one new process to enable them to work together productively.

1

Introduction

This chapter introduces three task-oriented group processes that are the "processes of choice" when helping a group to be more productive. They are useful ways to assist groups in conducting applied social research. The chapter includes sections on why the book focuses on these particular processes, what have been principal influences on the development and use of the three processes, why groups should be used to conduct applied social research, and what the advantages are of group wisdom versus individual leadership.

This book provides clear, complete, useful descriptions of selected task-oriented processes that the reader can use to help groups of people generate, develop, and select among ideas. The processes normally are used to enable small groups to address a specific planning or decision-making task and are often used in combination.

PROCESSES

Nominal Group Technique (NGT) is a method that allows individual judgments about a topic or issue to be pooled effectively. It is best used in small groups in which uncertainty or disagreement exists about the nature of a problem or possible solutions.

Ideawriting is a method for developing group ideas and exploring their meaning. It is particularly helpful in generating ideas and in making specific the general ideas that result from group interactions. Ideawriting focuses on a single topic, requires a relatively brief time, and produces a written product.

Interpretive Structural Modeling (ISM) is a method for identifying and summarizing relationships among specific items that define an issue or problem. ISM provides a means by which a group can impose order on the complexity of those items. The method is "interpretive" in that the group's judgment decides whether and how items are related. It is "structural" in that an overall structure is extracted from the complex set of items on the basis of the relationships. It is "modeling" in that the specific relationships and overall structure are portrayed in graphic form.

All three processes are formal responses to the group constraints of time, space, and personnel. Specific steps are followed in each process in order to overcome the problems that typically plague interacting groups. Therefore, the processes are presented didactically with emphasis on the stages of the techniques. For each process, stages or steps are identified that should be closely followed if the process is to be used effectively.

PROCESSES OF CHOICE

The processes—Nominal Group Technique, Ideawriting, and Interpretive Structural Modeling—are preferred above others because they are often the desirable way to circumvent the traditions and behaviors that interfere with group productivity. Nominal Group Technique is likely to produce a better product and a higher degree of group satisfaction than other ways of generating ideas, such as brainstorming. Ideawriting takes less time to address a topic than an interacting group and produces a written product that can be saved. Interpretive Structural Modeling enables a group to produce a dynamic outcome that is likely to be more useful to the group than typical ways of selecting among ideas, such as parliamentary procedure and voting.

The three processes are not substitutes for a very popular current group process called *focus groups*. Rather, they are tools that can be utilized to help achieve the goals of a focus group. A focus group is a method of using groups to gain insight. If, in order to gain insight about an idea, person, or product it is desirable to generate ideas, then NGT might be used. ISM could be a tool used to help make choices during a focus group.

PRINCIPAL INFLUENCES ON THE DEVELOPMENT AND USE OF THE PROCESSES

The study of group behavior is a relatively recent intellectual pursuit, confined essentially to the 20th century. The processes described in this book have become popular during the last 15 to 20 years. Nominal

Group Technique and Ideawriting are based on work in creativity, particularly on Osborne's work with brainstorming begun in the 1930s, but were introduced in print in 1975 by Delbecq and associates (Nominal Group Technique) and in 1976 by Warfield (Ideawriting). Interpretive Structural Modeling was introduced by Warfield in the early 1970s.

There are a number of convergent influences that help to explain the creation of and interest in using the processes. These influences are overlapping and interrelated; they are separated only so that they can be identified and described.

All of the processes were created in order to overcome problems that typically occur in groups. Nominal Group Technique was specifically designed to circumvent factors that have an adverse impact on groups, such as verbal aggressiveness and status; to enable groups to generate more alternatives than the limited number they would produce in a traditional interacting group; and to allow a group to be effective even if the members of the group do not know one another (Delbecq, Van de Ven, & Gustafson, 1975). Ideawriting controls the inhibiting influence on groups of verbal aggressiveness, provides people with the opportunity to phrase their thoughts clearly before speaking, and allows groups to have a permanent, rather than an ephemeral, record of their deliberations (Warfield, 1976). Interpretive Structural Modeling has as one of its goals the improvement of the quality of public debate by enabling a group to manage the complexity of ideas they have to consider (Warfield, 1976).

 I asked a group of expert facilitators, all of whom had experience working with the processes presented in this book, why processes such as NGT, Ideawriting, and ISM should be utilized in order to conduct applied social research. They contended that the use of such processes can improve the quality of virtually any kind of meeting (but particularly meetings between people who do *not* have a history of working together) by improving the group's productivity, eliminating confusion, promoting appreciation of the realities that need to be considered by the group, inventing alternatives, using time wisely, and circumventing many of the problems inherent in group activity. The problems they identified that these processes eliminate or reduce include when a group produces only a few ideas, when a group is dominated by one (or a few) of its members, when there is a lack of participation by all of the group members, when a group distorts its product because members respond too strongly to the status of one (or a few) of the group members, or when the group is unduly influenced by political problems (such as the authority of an elected chairperson or the established rules of procedure used to conduct meetings).

A basic tenet in applying the processes has been adopted from organizational development: Planning for organizational change should involve those who are likely to be affected by the change. The processes presented in this book facilitate the participation of a wide range of people by (a) helping reduce the influence that people of status have on the group's productivity (Who can be honest with the boss in the room?); (b) enabling a substantial amount of work to be accomplished in a brief time period (I cannot take the time away from my job for nonessential activities.); and (c) enabling people who do not have a history of working together to work effectively in groups.

During the 1960s and early 1970s a great deal of emphasis was placed on the socioemotional development of groups. Sensitivity training was big business. A variety of approaches to helping individuals and groups came to be called the *Human Potential Movement*. As a reaction against this movement and what its critics called the touchy-feely approach to groups, emphasis was placed on the development of processes that could help groups to become productive by accomplishing tasks. Thus, interest in the processes described in this book has been due at least in part to a reaction against what was perceived as the exclusive and excessive focus on group "health." Helping a group to accomplish its task often has the consequence of improving members' interpersonal relations and, consequently, the group's "health."

Professional problem solving traditionally has been predicated on the belief that select, well-trained individuals (experts) could analyze a problem and then apply their tools to solving the problem, virtually independent of those who had the problem. This view of professional problem solving was characterized by a set of assumptions, such as these:

- There is professional expertise that can be applied to other people's problems.

- The design process is a process wherein the professional [becomes informed] about a client's problems and then formulates a solution on the basis of . . . professional expertise.

- Any "publicizing" or exposure of the means by which decisions are reached is unnecessary because [a] professional is guided by [a] code of ethics.

- The development of increasingly complex techniques and procedures leads to better solutions, albeit at the cost of making the professional designer increasingly indispensable. (Olsen, 1982, p. 7)

Table 1.1
Comparison of Design Methods

First-Generation Methods	Second-Generation Methods
Process	
linear, sequential phasing of design activities	iterative activities carried out simultaneously
View of the Solution	
solution is fairly well defined at the outset	no clear-cut image of the solution
Methods	
scientific, systematic, quantitative, objective	systems, "political," participatory, holistic
Participants	
experts, specialists	participation by heterogeneous group of people (all with a stake or interest in the outcome)

In the early 1970s a different set of assumptions, called *second-generation design methods*, emerged. Some of the assumptions were:

- Expertise does not reside solely in the professional, but in all those who are affected by a design or planning problem.
- Planning and design should be viewed as an argumentative process or as a network of issues to be argued and decided.
- Any given issue can always be viewed as a symptom of some more fundamental one.
- A client who delegates judgment to a professional must be able to maintain control over the delegated judgment.
- The designer/planner conspires with his client to develop a solution, thus eliminating the problem of getting one's proposals implemented by his participation in producing the proposal. (Olsen, 1982, p. 9)

There are other important points of comparison between first- and second-generation design methods, as shown in Table 1.1.

The three processes presented in this book fall primarily within the assumptions of second-generation design methods because they typically are used to address ill-defined problems that require the participation of those who are (or will be) responsible for the problem and solution. An individual or group who is responsible for the solution is not likely to relinquish complete control over the process. Such a group is likely to be heterogeneous, particularly in terms of status—involving policy makers as well as those who have a direct stake in the outcome. Because the problem is ill defined, there is no clear-cut image of the solution.

Experts cannot solve such problems; they do not know enough (Lindblom & Cohen, 1979). Their analyses are opaque (often even to themselves). The direction of their findings is seldom unequivocal, their communication to policy makers—who must act on the knowledge that they have been provided—is seldom clear, and they are not accountable to any constituency for mistakes (Warfield, 1982).

John Warfield, when he was the director of the Center for Interactive Management within the School of Engineering and Applied Science at the University of Virginia, explained that the set of methodologies the Center used to address a given problem of management or planning must include at least one methodology that identifies problems, goals, and norms (*intelligence*); at least one that conceptualizes alternatives (*design*); and at least one that allows for the selection of the preferred alternative (*choice*). The processes presented in this book meet his criteria. Nominal Group Technique is essentially a way to generate ideas (intelligence), Ideawriting can be used to generate ideas but primarily is a way to develop ideas (design), and Interpretive Structural Modeling is a way to select ideas (choice).

USING GROUPS TO CONDUCT APPLIED SOCIAL RESEARCH

A book on group processes belongs in a series on applied social research. Whenever the conceptual work of research is conducted by a group or uses groups as sources of information, the three processes should be useful.

All of the processes can be used to answer research questions. You could use them to involve groups in answering questions such as:

What are the principal needs of the elderly in Kent, Ohio (as viewed by the elderly themselves; or as viewed by those of another demographic group)?

What do members of the legal profession perceive to be the issues that should be addressed by social science researchers?

Which work activities have priority for the county commissioners?
How can learning disabilities be characterized so that children can be grouped
   for instruction?

A common application of the processes is to facilitate the conduct of
research. Each of the processes can be used during the design of a
project; to clarify the focus of the project, to make choices about and
refine the use of data collection methods; and if there is a client, to
ensure that the design and projected product meet the client's expectations. They can be used during the implementation of a research project
to collect opinions and attitudes and to achieve consensus on topics or
issues. They can be used in the final stages of a research project to
generate recommendations for action based on the research results and
to establish priorities among the findings that need attention.

The processes may also serve as a research validation tool, to cor-
roborate and amplify data collected through a more quantitative approach. For example, you could use Ideawriting or the Nominal Group
Technique to systematically obtain the views of people to determine
whether the findings have face validity. The three processes, because
they reduce the disruptive impact on groups by people of high status
and encourage participation by everyone in the group, can be used
whenever it is desirable to collaborate in conducting research.

ADVANTAGES OF GROUP WISDOM
VERSUS INDIVIDUAL LEADERSHIP

The broader question, and one that is appropriate to ask, is why use
groups to address social problems? Why not simply carry out the vision
of a "leader"? The answer is in the wording of the question; "social"
problems exist because society functions in groups. As the group has
the problem, it is the group that must discover the solution that will work
for them.

Apart from this basic democratic tenet, there are at least four important reasons that make it desirable to use groups over individuals. First,
a group can do some things better than an individual. When it was
pointed out to Olaf Helmer, the inventor of the Delphi Technique, that
there is "no conclusive theoretical explanation why or how the Delphi
Technique does what it does," his response was that "it is logical that if
you properly combine the judgement of a large number of people, you

have a better chance of getting closer to the truth" (Helmer, 1981, p. 83). If you want to identify items for a test, develop an instrument, think through the implications of a research design, or discover the attitudes of a segment of the population, you are likely to do better if you use a group. After all, two or more heads are usually better than one: *pooled intelligence.*

The second reason to use groups is that *in order to understand social phenomena, it often is necessary to obtain the views of the actors.* Certain group processes, such as those presented in this book, enable the researcher to obtain the views of the critical actors. It is usually more desirable to ask citizens in a community what their needs are rather than depend on a review of the literature to tell you what they are likely to be. A literature review probably is going to provide you with generalizations that do not necessarily reflect a particular reality.

The third reason is that *it is often beneficial to use groups if you are concerned about the consequences of your research.* If your goal is to solve a problem of a particular group, it is reasonable to believe that the group is more likely to accept your advice (or research findings) if they have participated in the research process. This becomes a special issue when you are conducting applied social research that has political implications. (And virtually all important problems are likely to have substantial political consequences!) If you want to effect policy, it is wise to include those responsible for acting on the policy. Research on knowledge and research utilization has found that a critical factor in the usefulness and use of research is decision-maker involvement in the research process, which can only occur if there is communication between decision makers and researcher (e.g., Weiss, 1977). The group setting is the context for such communication.

The fourth reason is that *complex, ill-defined problems often can be addressed only by pooled intelligence.* Virtually all societal problems, which are the problems likely to be addressed by applied researchers, are complex, value laden, and ill defined (Olsen, 1982, p. 65; Strauch, 1974). Because societal problems are value laden, it is often appropriate to use groups to conduct applied social research. As explained earlier, this is especially true when it is necessary to involve the actors, either to obtain their knowledge and opinions or to assure the acceptance of the research effort. Groups may be used in conjunction with other research methods (e.g., a group could be used to help develop a questionnaire that would then be administered by a single researcher using traditional methods for conducting survey research) or may be the only approach taken by the applied researcher.

Quantitative research methods that identify and attempt to study variation in human behavior often are not suitable to address complex, ill-defined problems. The clearer the concept, the more it lends itself to quantification. As social problems become increasingly complex, they become more ill defined; quantification then becomes less useful.

SUMMARY

This book describes three task-oriented processes—Nominal Group Technique, Ideawriting, and Interpretive Structural Modeling—that are preferred ways to help groups of people generate, develop, and select among ideas. They help to circumvent the traditions and behaviors that interfere with group productivity.

Some of the principal influences on the development and use of these processes have been the desire to improve the productivity of interacting groups, the assumption of organizational development that people are responsible for solving their own problems, a preference for processes that help groups to accomplish tasks rather than help them feel good, the emergence of second-generation design methods that reflect less dependence on experts, and the need to use groups in order to manage the complexity of ideas.

Groups should be used to address social problems (a) because a group can do some things better than an individual, (b) in order to understand social phenomena it often is necessary to obtain the views of the actors, (c) because it often is beneficial to use groups if there is concern about the consequences of your research, and (d) because complex, ill-defined problems—those likely to be the focus of applied social researchers— often can be addressed only by pooled intelligence.

This book fits within a series on applied social research because the processes that it presents can be used to answer research questions, facilitate the conduct of research, serve as a research validation tool, and enable people to collaborate in conducting research.

2

Nominal Group Technique

This chapter describes Nominal Group Technique and includes sections on meeting preparations, the opening statement, conducting the NGT, and using NGT in a large group. An extended example of the technique, along with sections on limitations and resources, are also included. At the end of the chapter is an outline of NGT (called "At-a-Glance") and a detailed description of exactly what the reader could say and do if she or he were facilitating an NGT session.

Nominal Group Technique (NGT) is a method for structuring small group meetings that allows individual judgments about a topic or issue to be pooled effectively and used in situations in which uncertainty or disagreement exists about the nature of a problem and possible solutions. The process has been used extensively in business and government and has proven especially beneficial in fostering citizen participation in program planning.

The technique is helpful in identifying problems, exploring solutions, and establishing priorities. It works particularly well in "stranger groups," in which it is important to neutralize differences in status and verbal dominance among group members.

NGT typically includes four steps:

1. *Silent generation of ideas in writing*: Working silently and independently, participants jot down their responses to a stimulus question.
2. *Round-robin recording of ideas*: When called on, each participant contributes a single idea that is recorded on a large flip-chart. Discussion of the ideas is not permitted. Completed sheets are taped to the wall so that they can be seen by the group. The group facilitator continues to call on the participants until all ideas have been recorded or the group determines that they have produced a sufficient number of ideas.
3. *Serial discussion of the list of ideas*: The participants discuss each idea on the list so that they are clear about the meaning of the ideas.
4. *Voting*: The participants identify what each of them believes are the most important ideas, they rank-order their preferences, the votes are recorded on the flip-chart, and the voting pattern is discussed.

The ideal size of an NGT group is 5 to 9 members. Larger groups can be handled by making minor changes in procedure, particularly in Step 2 (see below), but any group larger than 12 or 13 should be divided. With an average-size group, the entire process can be comfortably completed in 75 minutes. By limiting Steps 2 and 3, it is possible for a group to go through the process in an hour.

THREE NGT ESSENTIALS

1. A carefully prepared question that evokes responses at the desired level of specificity.

2. A group of task-oriented individuals with expertise in the topic (do not be put off by the word *expertise*—citizens are expert on their needs; college students are expert on their tastes).

3. A group leader who has mastered the process and is willing to act as a process facilitator, not a substantive expert.

MEETING PREPARATIONS

There are four essential preparations that have to be made prior to the meeting by the group facilitator:

1. Formulate and test the NGT question: The facilitator should pay careful attention to the phrasing of the question. It should be as simple as possible, but it should elicit items at the desired level of specificity and abstraction. NGT is a single-question technique. A poor NGT question would be, "What are the goals to be achieved and the projects and programs to be undertaken by the city's community development program?" The question is poor because it is complex and, consequently, it will be difficult to analyze the ideas produced. A good NGT question would be, "What obstacles do you anticipate in carrying out the city's housing rehabilitation programs?"

Several people should be involved in preparing the question. They should begin by clarifying the objectives of the meeting. They should then illustrate the types of items they want to get from the group. With objectives and examples in mind, they can proceed to the composition of the question.

The NGT question should be pilot tested, if there is time, to make sure that it evokes the desired type of response. A propitious time for such testing is if the group is large and prospective group leaders will be trained to conduct NGT sessions.

2. *Assemble supplies,* including a flip-chart (or easel with newsprint or large sheets of paper—butcher-type paper or newspaper end-rolls that can be taped to the wall), water-based (rather than permanent) felt-tip pens that will not bleed through the paper, masking tape, and 3 × 5 cards for each group. The NGT question should be printed at the top of a sheet of paper and duplicated for each member.

3. *Prepare the meeting room:* Wall surfaces should be suitable for taping up sheets from the flip-chart. The best table arrangement is an open *U*, with the flip-chart located at the open end.

4. *Train inexperienced group leaders:* If the meeting will include more than 12 or 13 participants, and some or all of the group leaders have never conducted an NGT session, you should arrange a training session that simulates the process. For training purposes, good NGT questions are either the actual (or potential) question the group is planning to use or the general question, "What barriers do you anticipate in using NGT in your own organization (or agency or committee)?" If the actual question is used, the training session is an occasion to pilot test the phrasing of the NGT question.

OPENING STATEMENT

The opening statement is important because it can set the tone for the whole meeting. It should include at least three elements:

1. The importance of the task and the unique contributions of each group member should be noted.
2. The group should be informed of the session's overall goal and how the NGT results will be used.
3. The four basic steps of NGT should be briefly summarized.

When a large group is to be divided, it is best to present the opening statement at a plenary session before each NGT group begins its work. That way everyone will be operating under the same set of procedures.

CONDUCTING THE NGT

Step 1: Silent Generation of Ideas in Writing [4-8 minutes]

Distribute the question on individual sheets of paper or display it before the group. Read the question aloud to the group and ask members to respond to it by writing their ideas in phrases or brief sentences. Remind them that, because you will not be collecting their lists, good penmanship is unimportant.

Ask members to work silently and independently. Immediately stop disruptive behavior, such as talking.

> *HINT:* Demonstrate good behavior by doing your own silent writing.

Some members may ask about the meaning of the NGT question. You may illustrate the degree of abstraction desired or call on one of the members of the group to do so, but do not lead the group in any direction. Tell persistent questioners to respond to the NGT question in whatever way is most meaningful to them.

Allow 4 to 8 minutes for this step. In a large group, a short period of silent writing will appropriately limit the number of items the members produce. If there are multiple groups, it is desirable for the group leaders to agree in advance to allow the same amount of time for the silent generation of ideas in writing.

Step 2: Round-Robin Recording of Ideas [15-25 minutes]

Explain that the objective of this step is to collect the group's thinking. As you go around the table, each member is to present orally one idea from his or her own list in a phrase or brief sentence without discussion, elaboration, or justification. You will continue to go around the table until all ideas have been presented.

Explain that each member is to decide whether his or her item duplicates one already presented. A member may pass at any time, but may reenter the process later in his or her turn. Continue to call on members who have passed. Encourage members to "hitchhike" on others' ideas and to add new items, even though these items may not have been written down during Step 1.

The leader should record items on flip-chart sheets as rapidly as possible, numbering items in sequence and recording them in the members' own words. If possible, avoid condensing and abbreviating. It is very important that the participants know that they have produced the items and that the list belongs to them, not you. Ask long-winded participants to come up with simpler wording. If this causes delay, tell the person you will return for a shorter phrase and move on to the next member.

After you fill a sheet with numbered items, tape it to the wall where it will be visible to everyone. If you have someone to assist you, he or she can tape up the sheets while you continue with the round-robin recording. Another option that can expedite the process is to ask one of the group members to assist you by taping sheets to the wall.

With a large group, the length of the list can be controlled in several ways. For example, you can announce in advance that you will solicit items around the table only two or three times. Or, when a sufficient number of items have been generated, say that you will go around the table only once more and they should give you the best item remaining on their sheets.

Step 3: Serial Discussion of the Listed Ideas   [2 minutes/item]

Explain that the purpose of this step is to clarify the ideas presented. Read each item aloud in sequence and invite comments. Members may note their agreement or disagreement, but arguments are unnecessary as each person will vote independently in Step 4. Do not waste time on conflict. As soon as the logic of a position is clear, cut off discussion. The meaning of most items will be obvious to the group and little or no discussion will be necessary.

Announce in advance the number of minutes to be devoted to this step. The usual rule of thumb is to allot 2 minutes times the number of items. If time is short, allow only the number of minutes until adjournment, minus 15 minutes for the voting in Step 4.

Encourage viewing the list as group property. Anyone can clarify or comment on any item. If someone asks about the meaning of one of the items, it is productive to encourage someone other than the contributor of the particular item to clarify what it means to him or her. The group leader can model good behavior at an appropriate point with a comment such as, "Well, to me this item means . . ."

Within reason, new items can be added and small editorial changes made. Duplicate items may also be combined. However, the leader should resist attempts to combine many items into broader categories. Some members may seek to achieve consensus by this means, and the precision of the original items may be lost.

Step 4: Voting   **[15 minutes]**

Ranking is the simplest and usually most effective voting technique. Sometimes ratings are used, with each of the seven most important items on a list rated on a one-to-seven scale. Ranking is usually preferable, however, because it can be quickly tallied and the results are easily interpreted.

Each person should receive five 3 × 5 cards. Ask members to select the five most important items and write one in the center of each card. They should write the item's sequence number in the upper left corner. Tell them not to be concerned with penmanship; the only purpose for writing the item on the card is so that they will not have to refer back to the sheets on the wall when they rank-order their five cards.

> *HINT:* If the list includes more than 30 items, use seven cards rather than five.

```
17

Save the Whales
```

Give the group a time limit (4 or 5 minutes) for selecting its priority items and do a countdown (e.g., "You have 2 minutes left"). Request that the group members work silently, and that they wait until everyone is finished before rank-ordering the cards. Everyone will rank-order their choices together.

When everyone has completed the set of five cards, announce that the rank-ordering will begin. Go through the following instructions without delay, using this general wording.

> Spread the cards out in front of you so that you can see all five at once. Decide which card is more important than all the others. Put a 5 in the lower right-hand corner and underline it three times. Turn the card over.

```
 17

 Save the Whales

                                    5
                                    ‗
```

> Which is the least important of the four remaining cards? Put a 1 in the lower right corner and underline it three times. Turn the card over.
>
> Select the most important of the three remaining cards. Put a 4 in the lower right corner and underline it three times. Turn the card over.
>
> Select the least important of the two cards that are left. Put a 2 in the lower right corner and underline it three times.
>
> Put a 3 in the lower right corner of the last card and underline it three times.

Collect the cards and record the vote on the flip-chart in front of the group.

> *HINT:* When collecting the cards, shuffle them together to communicate to the participants that no one is going to pay attention to how each person voted.

You can prepare a tally sheet while the group is making their voting decisions.

VOTE

1.	13.
2.	14.
3.	15.
4.	16.
5.	17.
6.	18.
7.	19.
8.	20.
9.	21.
10.	22.
11.	23.
12.	24.

If someone is assisting you, ask them (or one of the members of the group) to read off the votes to you: "Item number 13 got a 3." The reason for having them underline their ranking three times is so that you can tell the difference between the number of the item and how they ranked the item. Tally rankings alongside the columns of item numbers. The example below shows how a group of six members voted on a list of 24 items.

VOTE

1. *2,1,1,1*	13. *3,3*
2.	14. *4*
3. *5,4,5,5,3,4*	15.
4. *3,2*	16.
5. *5*	17. *4,3,3,1*
6.	18. *2*
7. *5*	19. *1*
8.	20.
9. *2*	21. *4*
10. *1*	22.
11. *2*	23.
12. *5,4,2*	24.

Lead a discussion of the voting pattern. The number of votes an item gets is likely to be the most important indication of its relative priority.

Resist the temptation to play numerical games, such as adding the rankings together to arrive at a consolidated score. In the above example, adding the scores would obscure the different patterns of support for items 1 and 5: that four different members of the group thought that item 1 was one of their most important items.

It is usually worthwhile for the group to consider whether there are any themes that the items cluster within. If time permits, the group can further clarify the items and vote again. Keep the discussion brief, and caution people not to change their minds frivolously.

USING NGT IN A LARGE GROUP

With a large group, begin with a plenary session at which you present the opening statement. Then divide the group into subgroups of five to nine persons and conduct simultaneous NGT sessions. Separate meeting rooms are preferable, but it is possible to separate people in one large room if the acoustics and wall space are suitable.

Often a large group meeting will be finished as soon as the individual NGT groups have produced their product. The groups may come together for a plenary session at which each of the small groups report their results and a monitoring group will then be responsible for analyzing the products that have been generated. Occasionally the group will want to consolidate the separate products before they leave. Their goal usually is to produce one single, prioritized list that represents the work of the full group.

Consolidating Lists

It may be desirable to consolidate the lists of each subgroup. Allow at least 90 minutes (2 hours is better) for the group facilitators to meet and create a master list. The participants should be occupied elsewhere with a plenary session of some type, such as a luncheon or a panel discussion.

An efficient procedure for consolidating lists is to begin with each group facilitator describing the items that received the strongest support in the group's voting. Through discussion, the facilitators will agree on two types of strongly supported items: (a) duplicate items that should be reworded and (b) items unique to a single group. The latter can be transferred with only minor editing to the master list. The former require much more care in rewording because you are trying to reflect the meanings of different groups with one statement.

Plenary Session Voting

The master list is likely to have between 15 and 25 items, a manageable size for discussion. It should be written on flip-chart sheets and placed on the wall of the meeting room. The group then reassembles in plenary session. A facilitator leads a serial discussion of the master list in order to clarify the meaning of each item and to add items if desired. The group should be given a number of opportunities to add items that they believe were important in their small group session but that have been left off of the consolidated list. Otherwise, the participants will become suspicious that an attempt has been made to manipulate the list. The group then votes as in Step 4. The vote is tabulated and displayed before the group.

AN EXAMPLE

The political leaders of a rural region, composed of three counties that encompass an Indian tribe and numerous governmental entities, were preparing to negotiate with the state and federal governments. Their goal was to improve the region by obtaining legislative and financial concessions. Before a credible proposal could go forward, it was necessary for the leaders of the area to be able to describe what the citizens desired.

The decision was made to hold a community-wide meeting to ascertain the desires of the citizens. First, it was necessary to have a planning meeting in order to build the agenda for the community meeting and to identify who should be invited to the meeting. Nominal Group Technique was used in order to accomplish the latter task.

Seven people and a facilitator sat around an oval-shaped table in a small conference room. All of them had been asked to attend the meeting because they were knowledgeable community leaders and were interested in the ultimate success of the project. The facilitator reminded them why they were there and what they had to accomplish. He summarized the steps of the NGT process and then passed out a sheet of paper to each person with the following question at the top of the page: What are the criteria that should be met in order to assure that the community meeting is truly representative?

He gave the group 4 minutes to jot down ideas in response to that question. He made it clear that he would not be picking up the papers, but that they were work sheets for group members to use as they saw fit. After the time was up, he went around the table and asked each of the participants to contribute one criterion, which he wrote on newsprint. As he filled each sheet of newsprint, he taped it to the wall so that it could be viewed by the whole group. The group generated 18 criteria. The facilitator then read each criterion in order and asked the group to question any of the criteria that were not clear to them. After that serial discussion, which led to a consolidation of a few of the criteria, a voting procedure was used to identify which of the criteria the group thought were most important. First, they each selected what they thought were the five most important criteria and wrote each of them on separate 3 × 5 cards. Second, they were led through a procedure that allowed each of them to rank-order their five preferences. All of the cards were collected and tallied. A discussion of the vote resulted in the group's agreement on what should be the criteria.

After a break, the group was asked to take about 10 minutes and to write down on a sheet of paper the names of people who met the criteria and would make a substantial contribution to the community meeting. While the group was working silently and independently, the facilitator placed single sheets of paper on the wall with one criterion on each sheet. When the 10 minutes were up, he passed out large index cards to each of the participants. As he called on each of the participants, he asked them to recommend a name, to print the name on one of the index cards, and to suggest which of the criteria that person met. He then taped the recommended name on the wall beneath the appropriate criterion.

After the names were up on the wall, the group discussed the suitability of the list. They suggested additional names where there appeared to be gaps and reduced the number where there were too many in a category.

The meeting ended with each person present being assigned different responsibilities (such as arranging for the meeting site, drafting the letter of invitation, contacting certain potential participants, and mailing out the invitations) for conducting the community meeting.

One of the decisions made at the planning meeting was that NGT would be a suitable process to use at the community meeting in order to enable the citizens to identify the needs of the community. The facilitator determined that it would be most productive if local citizens ran the NGT sessions at the community meeting. Therefore, a training session was planned in order to prepare selected citizens to play that role.

The training session, held the day before the community meeting, lasted 2 hours. Eight persons learned how to conduct an NGT by participating in a session that simulated what would be done the following day. They even used the same NGT question, which provided an opportunity to test whether or not the question elicited the desired results. After the simulated session, the facilitator debriefed the prospective group leaders.

The community meeting began with presentations on why the group was meeting and what some of the critical issues facing the region were. Seven groups, with 9 to 14 members each, used NGT to address the following question: What issues, problems, and opportunities should be addressed in order to make the region a better place to live in the 1980s? (This appears to be a complex question rather than the preferred simple question. However, it was explained to those in attendance that they may have different orientations; some may think in terms of issues, others in terms of problems, and others may see issues or problems as opportunities. The purpose of the small group sessions was to capture all of their ideas.)

During a lunch break, the NGT group leaders met in order to create a composite list of the items that had a high priority in each of the separate groups. When the full group reconvened, the composite list was presented. Members discussed each of the items (for purposes of clarification), modified the language of some of the items, and added items that they thought had priority in their small group but had been left off of the composite list.

They then voted on which of the items on the composite list should have priority.

A report was prepared and distributed to all those who attended the meeting. The ideas generated at the community meeting became the input for additional planning meetings and substantially influenced what were designated as the priorities in planning for the region.

LIMITATIONS

NGT is easy to learn and use. Moreover, groups enjoy participating in an NGT because they realize they have been unusually productive in a relatively brief time. Consequently, the process is seductive. Because it is easy to use and accomplishes a great deal, there is a tendency to overuse it. After awhile, all problems seem as if they can be addressed by NGT. As one of its benefits is its novelty—groups are "tricked" into being more productive than they would be if they did not use the process—repeated use may have a dampening effect on a participant. NGT may also be used in ways that are inappropriate. The process is not suitable for all questions and all groupings of people. People accustomed to getting their way in groups, including highly verbal people like some politicians, may even resist participation in an NGT. Once they realize they cannot control the outcome as they are accustomed to doing, they are likely to try to modify the process. They will claim that NGT is a game or is sophomoric. Those accustomed to being assisted by staff may also be uncomfortable about participation in an NGT.

NGT includes a voting procedure and, therefore, gives the impression that the final product represents a group consensus. The NGT vote may be final—the group might act according to the vote—but usually the principal outcome is the generation of ideas. The vote is simply a way to bring closure to the group's activity and does suggest the group's preferences. The vote is helpful when there are multiple groups (and there is a desire to consolidate the high-priority ideas from each of the groups) or when there is a plan to use another process—such as Idea-writing or ISM—to develop the ideas suggested by NGT.

Although the ideas generated in an NGT are more developed than those that emerge during a simple brainstorming session, they are still only suggestive. In fact, the product of an NGT session is not usually clear to an external audience that did not participate in the session. Moreover, the quality of the ideas is likely to vary greatly. Some may be shallow, uninformed, or impractical. Therefore, NGT is usually a starting place and needs to be used in conjunction with a process for idea development.

The following statement was made in response to the ideas that emerged out of the community meeting example presented above. It illustrates the tentative nature of the ideas produced by one NGT conference. Recall that the ideas from a number of NGT sessions were consolidated into a single list and considered by the full group. The NGT question was: "What issues, problems, and opportunities should be addressed in order to make the region a better place to live in the 1980s?"

The goals as developed were at a very general level. They actually mixed together *topics* (e.g., community planning) with *solutions* (e.g., a new rural water system) with *questions* (e.g., how can we get the Feds to change ill-fitting policies?). More importantly, general statements tend to mask differences. When they become more specific, general concepts which we all favor (such as low-income housing and abundant clean water) can lead to many different perceptions about what is really needed to make individuals happy. In the process of specifying concrete objectives, it is also important to make clear the relationship between a problem and a solution. In many programs, they are not as tightly connected as they need to be. (Williams, 1980, p. A1)

This limitation is a principal reason why participants in an NGT session need to understand how the NGT product will be used. If possible, the participants need to be apprised of the full project and how their participation fits within the project.

Time is usually a constraint on a group, and that influences the NGT steps. The goal of Step 3 is to clarify ideas. The relative merit of the ideas could be discussed and argued, but that takes considerably more time. Moreover, it is likely to put the group into an interacting mode and allow some people to dominate the proceedings. However, if it is necessary (or even appropriate) for the group to consider the relative merit of the ideas, schedule sufficient time for that to occur.

RESOURCES

Nominal Group Technique was invented in 1968 by Andre Delbecq and Andrew Van de Ven. The most comprehensive description can be found in Delbecq, Van de Ven, and Gustafson (1975). Delbecq and Sandra Gill have a chapter on NGT in Olsen (1982, pp. 271-287).

APPENDIX 2.1
Presenting NGT Results

The following is a partial example of how to present the results of a typical NGT session.

NGT question: What issues, problems, and opportunities should be addressed in order to make the region a better place to live in the 1980s?

Votes	Items
2, 1, 1, 1	(1) Maintain and develop natural and human resources; creation of industry and jobs.
	(2) Development of educational resources: funding base, curriculum, facilities.
5, 4, 5, 4, 3, 4	(3) Reduce dependency on federal funds; develop own resources.
3, 2	(4) Adequate water treatment and sewage facilities.
5	(5) County government underfunded.
	(6) Strong program to induce probusiness legislation and reform. Effect change in political process.

NGT-AT-A-GLANCE

Meeting Preparation

- Formulate and test the NGT question.
- Assemble equipment (flip-chart) and supplies (water-based markers, masking tape, index cards).
- Prepare the meeting room.
- Train inexperienced leaders. [optional]

Opening Statement

Inform the participants of the context of the session, indicate how the NGT results will be used. Announce the four basic NGT steps.

Conducting the NGT Process

1. Silent Generation of Ideas in Writing [4-8 minutes]

Have the question legibly printed on the first sheet of flip-chart paper. Distribute a sheet of paper with the question at the top of the sheet. Read the question aloud and ask members to list their responses in phrases or brief sentences. Request that they work silently and independently.

2. Round-Robin Recording of Ideas [15-25 minutes]

Go around and get one idea from each group member. Write the ideas on sheets of flip-chart paper. As you finish each sheet, tape it on the wall so that it is visible to the group. Encourage hitchhiking on other ideas. Do not allow discussion, elaboration, or justification.

3. Serial Discussion of the List of Ideas [2 minutes/item]

Explain that the purpose of this step is clarification. Read Item 1 aloud and invite comments. Then read Item 2, and continue discussing each item in turn until the list is covered. Arguments are unnecessary because each member will have a chance to vote independently in Step 4. As soon as the logic of a position is clear, move on to the next item.

4. Voting [15 minutes]

Each person selects the five items (or more, depending on the number of items generated) that are most important and writes each on a 3×5 card. These are then rank-ordered. The votes are recorded on the flip-chart in front of the group. The group discusses the voting pattern. If desired, the items can be further clarified and a second vote taken.

NGT FROM THE PERSPECTIVE
OF THE READER AS FACILITATOR

The following is a step-by-step illustration of Nominal Group Technique (NGT) and how to facilitate one. Ideally, a chairperson (or the equivalent) will clarify the purpose for the meeting, the context for the meeting (how this meeting fits into the history of the group and their ongoing work), and your (the facilitator's) role. You should be prepared to describe your role if it is not done by someone else. Outline the steps in the NGT. You might say something like:

Given the session's purpose, I propose the following:

First, everyone will work silently and independently for 4 minutes. You should take that time to jot down all of the responses you can think of to the question.

Next, I will go around the table, calling on you one at a time so you can give one of your ideas. I will write them down on the wall sheets. I will go around the table a number of times, at least until I get down most of the ideas each of you have written during the silent work.

After I have recorded your ideas, we will revisit each one of them in order to make certain that its meaning is clear for everyone in the group.

The final step will be a voting procedure whereby the people in the group identify what they believe are the best responses to the question.

Then ask the group, "Do those four steps appear to you to be a reasonable way for the group to get its work done?"

Pass out sheets of paper with the triggering question at the top of the page. Tell the group:

For the next 4 minutes, please work silently and independently. The paper is for jotting down ideas. It will not be collected.

If anyone does start to talk or to do anything else that is likely to be disruptive to the others in the group, remind them:

This is the time for each of you to do your own work. You will get a chance to talk to the other members of the group in just a moment.

HINT: During the time that the group is working silently, tear off masking tape for hanging wall sheets and sort index cards into groups of five for the voting. This could have been done before the meeting. You will need one group of cards for each participant.

After the group has finished silently writing, begin the collection of ideas. You might begin by saying something like:

I want to go around the table and collect one idea at a time from each of you. I will call on each of you more than once, so you will have a chance to contribute at least a few of your ideas.

Listen to what others in the group say, to make certain that you do not give me exactly the same idea. I do not need to write down an idea more than once. Another reason to listen is because someone may say something that causes you to remember something that should be contributed and you might not have thought about it had you not listened.

You may pass at any time if you do not have an item to contribute when I call on you. I will call on you again when I come back to you the next time.

As an item is given to you, record it on the flip-chart. Write down exactly what they say. Do not ask them to say it in a few words (unless it is extremely long). Resist the temptation to say, "Don't you really mean . . ." and then provide your idea. It is very important that the group feel that it is their list, and the most important thing that can be done to assure they believe that the list is theirs is to use their language. Number each item in consecutive order.

> *HINT:* Alternate the colors of each item. That will
> enhance the readability of the items.

Speed is the most important factor in getting down the items. Do not belabor your handwriting or worry about your spelling. Get the items down quickly.

You should collect all of their items, if possible. But there is a point of diminishing return if the list gets too long. Experience suggests that a list of 20 to 30 will include almost all of a group's important items. If it is a very large group, 12 or more, tell them that you are going to go around the group two times. That will encourage them to give you their best items. After two passes, you can ask if there are any more items that have to be on the list. If it is a very, very large group, 25 or more, and you were not able to do the best thing, which would have been to break them up into more than one group, you should not try to go around the group more than once.

When all of the ideas have been collected and are written down on sheets in front of the group, the task is to clarify the meaning of the ideas. The way to do this is to read each of them, in order, and ask if the meaning of the item is clear. If it is, if there are no comments about the meaning of the item, move on to the next one. Do that until you work your way through the entire list. You need to be clear with the group that this is not an occasion to argue about the worth of an item. They will have an opportunity in the next stage, with their vote, to indicate which items they believe are most important.

There are occasions when it is important for the group to argue about the worth of the items on the list, but only if they have allocated sufficient time to do that. Your job as facilitator will be to keep the group to the time they have allocated.

One suggestion for how to allocate time is to allow 15 minutes for voting and to divide the remaining time by the number of items. For example, if you have an hour left at the point when you are about to begin discussing the items, that will give you 45 minutes for the discussion. If you have 20 items to consider, you might announce to the group that they have a little over 2 minutes to discuss each item.

It is often the case that someone will try to reduce the complexity of the list by grouping items in broad categories. Your rule should be to consider such a request only if the items are identical. Someone gave you the item with the knowledge they were only to contribute it if it was different. Sometimes group discussion can determine that two (or even more) items mean the same thing, and you should do something about that, such as create a single item and eliminate the duplicates. But make changes in the list very cautiously and with respect for the original language. Check with the group. Ask them, "Do items 6 and 11 mean exactly the same thing?" If not, allow them to stay in their original form.

Once the group is clear about the meaning of the items, they can vote to determine which are the most important items. Pass out five 3 × 5 index cards to each person and then instruct them as follows:

> I am going to give you 4 minutes to identify the five most important items and to put one on each card. Put the number of the item in the upper left-hand corner of the card and put the actual wording of the item in the middle of the card.

> *HINT:* It is a good idea to illustrate what you want by putting a sample on a wall sheet.

```
17

Save the Whales
```

After they have completed the task of selecting their five items, continue with:

> Now that you have identified the five most important items, lay them out in front of you so that you can see all five at once. Select the most important one of the five, put 5 in the lower right-hand corner, underline it, and turn that card over.

Again, it is helpful to illustrate what you want.

> Now select the least important of the five items, give it a 1, underline it, and turn that card over.
>
> Of the remaining three cards, pick the most important one, give it a 4, underline it and turn it over.
>
> Of the remaining two cards, pick the least important one, give it a 2, underline it, and turn it over.
>
> The last item should get a 3. Underline the 3 and turn the cards in to me.

Tabulate the vote.

> **HINT:** While they are selecting their five items there is an opportunity for you to prepare a vote sheet, which is a sheet that says *vote* at the top and has two columns of numbers that reflect the number of items that the group generated.

The following is an example from a group that had generated 24 items.

VOTE

1.	13.
2.	14.
3.	15.
4.	16.
5.	17.
6.	18.
7.	19.
8.	20.
9.	21.
10.	22.
11.	23.
12.	24.

Ask for a volunteer from the group to assist you by calling off from the cards the number of the item and the vote that it received. You then place the vote beside the appropriate number. Do that until all of the votes have been tabulated. The following is an example of how a group vote might look.

VOTE

1. *2,1,1,1*	13. *3,3*
2.	14. *4*
3. *5,4,5,5,3,4*	15.
4. *3,2*	16.
5. *5*	17. *4,3,3,1*
6.	18. *2*
7.	19. *1*
8. *5*	20.
9. *2*	21. *4*
10. *1*	22.
11. *2*	23.
12. *5,4,2*	24.

Discuss the vote. You might give the group a short break while you are tabulating the vote. They will probably take a break on their own, even if you do not tell them to do it. After the vote is tabulated, reconvene them, identify the items that got the largest number of votes, and ask them to tell you what the vote means. Often it is appropriate at this point to cluster items to indicate patterns in the vote. Your responsibility to the group is now complete. Someone in charge, such as a chairperson, should take over the meeting and discuss the next steps with the group.

3

Ideawriting

This chapter describes Ideawriting and includes sections on meeting preparations, the opening statement, and conducting the Ideawriting process. Two examples of Ideawriting, along with sections on limitations and resources, are also included. At the end of the chapter is an outline of Ideawriting (called "At-a-Glance") and a detailed description of exactly what the reader could say and do if she or he were facilitating an Ideawriting session.

Ideawriting, a group method for developing ideas and exploring their meaning, is particularly helpful in making more specific the general ideas that result from group interactions. Another valuable use of Ideawriting is idea generation.

Ideawriting typically includes four steps:

1. *Group organization*: A large group is divided into small working groups.

2. *Initial response*: Each participant reacts in writing to a stimulus question or item and then places his or her Ideawriting form (with the initial response) in the center of the group.

3. *Written interaction*: Each participant reacts, in writing, to what is written on each of the other Ideawriting forms.

4. *Analysis and reporting*: Each participant reads the comments made in reaction to his or her initial response, the small working group discusses the principal ideas that emerge from the written interaction, and the group summarizes the discussion on newsprint.

Ideawriting focuses on a single topic, requires a relatively brief time, and produces a written product. The process recognizes that (a) certain group goals can be achieved best by writing rather than by discussion, (b) parallel working (each of the members of the group work on the same task at the same time) is productive and efficient, and (c) all members of a group should be allowed an equal opportunity to express their ideas. The process is quite useful when the group is large, the meeting schedule allocates a limited time for group discussion, or differences among group members (in status and verbal aggressiveness) need to be neutralized.

An important advantage of Ideawriting is that one leader can facilitate the work of a large number of Ideawriting groups. This means that the technique is useful for larger conferences or meetings. An Ideawriting session can easily be accomplished in an hour, and an abbreviated version in a half hour.

CAUTION

Do not use Ideawriting unless the participants are willing to express themselves in writing. The legibility of the writing is not usually an issue, but if participants are self-conscious about their ability to write, they may not cooperate or they may even disrupt the process.

MEETING PREPARATIONS

First, decide whether the group task requires that all members respond to the same stimulus, such as a common question, or whether members should select the item they prefer from a list of alternatives. If a single triggering question is used as the stimulus to the group activity, formulate and if possible test the question. An example of an appropriate question would be, "What is an effective strategy for generating additional jobs in the private sector?"

If the group members are to respond to a set of stimulus items, write those items on newsprint so that they can be displayed before the group. For example, the group might have a previously prepared list of potential strategies for generating additional jobs in the private sector. If so, write the list on sheets of newsprint and tape them to the wall. The question for this group might be, "What are critical considerations that must be taken into account in implementing any one of the potential strategies?"

Second, assemble necessary supplies: pads of paper, pencils, pens, tables, and chairs. If the groups are to analyze and report their results, at least one flip-chart (or easel), newsprint, masking tape, and water-based (rather than permanent) felt-tip pens should also be available. Ideally, each Ideawriting group should have a separate table around which to sit.

OPENING STATEMENT

Briefly:

1. Stress the importance of the task.
2. State how the results will be used.
3. Summarize the basic steps of the Ideawriting process. Present the steps on a sheet of newsprint and/or on the Ideawriting form.
4. Special reminders:
   (a) Note that the writing should be done silently.
   (b) Tell the participants not to worry about their writing (style, spelling, or punctuation). Suggest that they may write in phrases, rather than sentences. The emphasis is on ideas, not wording.
   (c) Explain that the initial response to the question should take about 5 minutes, the silent writing phase should be completed in about 10 minutes, and the analysis and reporting should take about 10 minutes.

CONDUCTING THE IDEAWRITING PROCESS

Step 1: Group Organization

If the group is large, divide it into small groups of three or four persons. You might ask one person in each small group to serve as the group leader. If you do, charge the leaders with the responsibility of seeing to it that the groups follow the steps of the process. In a very large group, you might ask them to count off and then designate all the number "ones" as leaders. The key is to have someone in each group responsible for an orderly expeditious process.

Step 2: Initial Response   [5 minutes]

If the group is responding to a triggering question, members should write their names in the upper right-hand corner, write the triggering question in the space provided on the Ideawriting form, and briefly list their responses to the question (see Figure 3.1).

If the group is responding to a set of stimulus items (e.g., sheets of newsprint on the wall with strategies), members should write their names in the upper right-hand corner, select and write one item (e.g., one of the strategies) in the space provided, and write their responses

IDEAWRITING

STEP ONE: <u>INITIAL IDEAS</u>   [approximately 5 minutes]
(Leave plenty of room around and between ideas)

STEP TWO: <u>WRITTEN INTERACTION</u>   [approximately 10 minutes]

    o Select a sheet other than your own.

    o Read the ideas and or comments.

    o Write down your reactions.
      -Which do you like?
      -Which do you dislike?
      -What else can you think of?
      -How could each idea be improved?

    o Read and react to each idea writing sheet.

STEP THREE: <u>DISCUSSION</u>   [approximately 10 minutes]

    o Read your original ideas and the comments.

    o Conduct a discussion of the principal ideas
      from all the sheets

    o Record ideas on a single piece of newsprint.

QUESTION:

INITIAL IDEAS:

Figure 3.1. Ideawriting Form With Instructions

to the item. It may be useful to assign items. Otherwise, let each member select whichever item interests him or her the most. This alternative may result in duplicate items, but experience suggests that a variety of ideas will be developed.

Step 3: Written Interaction   [10 minutes]

Members should place their Ideawriting forms in the center of the table. They should select a form other than their own and briefly respond to what is on the paper by adding written comments. It is appropriate to offer solutions, qualify what is written, add suggestions, and criticize weaknesses. Each person should return the Ideawriting form to the center of the table. Repeat this process until each member has responded to every other member's ideas.

Step 4: Analysis and Reporting   [10 minutes]

The following steps should be followed to analyze the work and report the results.

- Members should read the comments on their Ideawriting forms and orally report them for the other members of their small group. The ideas can then be discussed and summarized.
- It is advisable that each of the small groups summarize its efforts on a single sheet of newsprint as the sheets provide an efficient way to report back to the large group once it reconvenes.
- The group should appoint one of its members (perhaps the assigned group leader) to report the general findings of the group's work to the large group.
- At the large group session, the representatives from each small group should report on the group's ideas, perhaps by explaining the sheet of newsprint.
- If time permits, the large group can then discuss the ideas.

AN EXAMPLE

A mayor appointed a task force of 15 persons to recommend actions that city government and local business firms could take to cope with a chronically high unemployment rate. Having decided to use Ideawriting as a method for generating and refining recommendations, the chairperson prepared for the first meeting by drafting a triggering question to which everyone would respond: What can the public and private sectors in this community do to reduce unemployment? When the task force convened, the chairperson explained the purpose of the group and how the mayor was likely to use its report. The chairperson read the question and proposed Ideawriting as the best way to tap the experience and judgment of every member. After describing the process and securing the group's agreement to try it, the chairperson divided the task force into five 3-member groups. Someone in each group was asked to make sure that the Ideawriting proceeded smoothly.

Each group sat around a small table, out of earshot of the others. The few last-minute questions about the process were briefly discussed and clarified. Then a silent writing phase began.

Individually, group members wrote their last names and the triggering question on an Ideawriting form. Next, everyone responded to the question by writing a few ideas. Members were free to respond in any way they wished. Some provided short lists of alternatives; others described the important characteristics of a single action. One person stated why, in his judgment, the group was dealing with the wrong question.

After the initial response, members placed their Ideawriting forms in the center of the table, took the form of another group member, read what the other had written, and wrote a few comments in response. Again, a wide variety of responses were made. Many members were stimulated to add new alternative actions. Some identified potential problems with other members' suggestions or pointed out how a particular proposal could be implemented. Still others indicated which of the suggested actions had the greatest promise in the short run.

The process of alternatively reading and writing ideas continued in silence until each person had commented on the ideas of all other group members. When the originators got their Ideawriting forms back, they contained three brief statements, only the first of which was written by them. In this fashion, each of the small groups produced three sets of suggested actions, as well as critiques of those actions. An Ideawriting Form looked something like Figure 3.2.

After the silent writing was over, members read what was on their Ideawriting forms and summarized them orally for the rest of the group. The group discussed and synthesized the major ideas, writing them on a sheet of newsprint. The task force reconvened to hear reports from all five groups. The chairperson used the newsprint summaries to assign topics to committees for additional study.

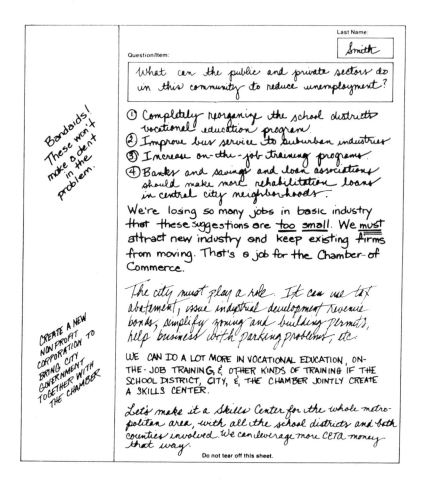

Figure 3.2. Sample Ideawriting Page

ANOTHER EXAMPLE

The following example illustrates one of the advantages of Ideawriting—that one person can facilitate the work of a large number of people.

Approximately 700 people participated in an Ideawriting session at an international conference. The purpose of the session (to introduce the participants to techniques that are useful for thinking about the future, as well as to generate some ideas on a particular topic) and the steps in the process were briefly outlined at a general assembly for all of the participants. The full group then subdivided into four groups. The participants in the four groups sat at tables with approximately 8 to 10 persons per table. Three common activities were followed by each table:

1. The tables established subgroups of 4 to 5 persons per group.
2. Each subgroup was assigned a goal. The following are examples of the goals they were assigned.

   (a) Reduce Energy Consumption

   (b) Use Public Sector Resources More Efficiently

   (c) Provide a Range of Public Community Facilities

3. Each subgroup used Ideawriting in the following manner.

   (a) They placed their stimulus question at the top of their Ideawriting form. An example would be, "How can we plan and construct buildings and development projects so that we *reduce energy consumption?*" The question was the same for everyone, only the goals (e.g., reduce energy consumption) differed.

   (b) Ten minutes were allotted for each participant to respond independently to the question.

   (c) Twenty minutes were allowed for the participants to engage in written interaction. Each of them selected a form other than her own, read it, and reacted to it by writing additional comments. The process was repeated until everyone had responded to every other person's ideas.

   (d) Each subgroup summarized their Ideawriting work by having each individual read the sheet she initiated and then by discussing the ideas. Each table identified the five most promising options, ideas, characteristics, or plans.

   (e) Each table then completed one *impact analysis* matrix (Figure 3.3) by

   • filling in, across the top of the matrix, the five most promising options,

   • making a group judgment (a show of hands was sufficient) about the extent to which each option facilitated the achievement of each of the goals. They used the following symbols:

       + = beneficial impact

       − = detrimental impact

       ✓ = uncertain or mixed impact

       0 = no likely impact, and

   • completing each box in the matrix by circling the most applicable of the four symbols.

   (f) Each table then examined the matrix in order to identify those options that seemed to have a beneficial impact on most of the goals.

IMPACT ANALYSIS

INSTRUCTIONS:

+ beneficial impact
− detrimental impact
✓ uncertain or mixed impact
0 no likely impact

Each table should complete one IMPACT ANALYSIS matrix by doing the following:

ɸ Fill in, across the top of the matrix, the 5 most promising options identified by your group.

ɸ Make a group judgment about the extent to which each option facilitates the achievement of each of the goals. Use the symbols, +, −, ✓, and 0 (defined at left).

ɸ Complete each box in the matrix below for each goal by circling the most applicable of the 4 symbols.

Fill in the Options → Goals ↓	Option 1	Option 2	Option 3	Option 4	Option 5
A. Reduce energy consumption	+ − ✓ 0	+ − ✓ 0	+ − ✓ 0	+ − ✓ 0	+ − ✓ 0
B. Use public sector resources more efficiently	+ − ✓ 0	+ − ✓ 0	+ − ✓ 0	+ − ✓ 0	+ − ✓ 0
C. Provide a range of public community facilities	+ − ✓ 0	+ − ✓ 0	+ − ✓ 0	+ − ✓ 0	+ − ✓ 0
D. Use private sector resources more carefully	+ − ✓ 0	+ − ✓ 0	+ − ✓ 0	+ − ✓ 0	+ − ✓ 0
E. Facilitate economic development	+ − ✓ 0	+ − ✓ 0	+ − ✓ 0	+ − ✓ 0	+ − ✓ 0
F. Contain housing and development costs	+ − ✓ 0	+ − ✓ 0	+ − ✓ 0	+ − ✓ 0	+ − ✓ 0
G. Facilitate social and economic mobility	+ − ✓ 0	+ − ✓ 0	+ − ✓ 0	+ − ✓ 0	+ − ✓ 0
H. Meet the needs of diverse households	+ − ✓ 0	+ − ✓ 0	+ − ✓ 0	+ − ✓ 0	+ − ✓ 0
I. Provide a high level of private amenities	+ − ✓ 0	+ − ✓ 0	+ − ✓ 0	+ − ✓ 0	+ − ✓ 0
J. Maintain the benefits of accessibility	+ − ✓ 0	+ − ✓ 0	+ − ✓ 0	+ − ✓ 0	+ − ✓ 0
K. Maintain private sector motivation	+ − ✓ 0	+ − ✓ 0	+ − ✓ 0	+ − ✓ 0	+ − ✓ 0
L. Maintain existing environmental standards	+ − ✓ 0	+ − ✓ 0	+ − ✓ 0	+ − ✓ 0	+ − ✓ 0

Figure 3.3. Impact Analysis Page With Instructions

A spokesperson for each of the four groups reported to the general assembly when the full group reconvened. The Ideawriting process, including filling in the impact analysis, took approximately 90 minutes. One person facilitated the work in each of the four rooms, so that there were four facilitators for 700 participants.

LIMITATIONS

As the demands of facilities and supplies are not great, there are few limitations on the use of Ideawriting. The principal limitation would be the group that is participating in the process; it is imperative that they be willing to express themselves in writing. One should not be hesitant about using Ideawriting with a group of professionals, but should be cautious about using the process with a group of citizens or even elected officials. These groups may be suitable, but the burden falls on the group leader to make that assessment.

RESOURCES

There are few printed references to Ideawriting, other than John Warfield (1976), who refers to it as "brainwriting," and Thissen, Sage, and Warfield (1980).

IDEAWRITING AT-A-GLANCE

Meeting Preparation

- Formulate and test trigger question or stimulus items.
- Assemble supplies (newsprint, pads of paper, water-based markers, masking tape).
- Prepare sheets of newsprint with stimulus items at top.
- Divide large group into smaller groups of three or four people.

Opening Statement

Stress the importance of the task and how the results will be used. Announce the three basic Ideawriting steps. Remind the group that writing should be done silently and that they should not be concerned about their writing or spelling, as long as it is legible. Explain the time expectations. Pass out the Ideawriting form.

Conducting the Ideawriting Process

1. Initial Response   [5 minutes]

Each person should write their name and the triggering question or stimulus item in the appropriate place on the Ideawriting form. Working silently and independently in small groups of three or four, each person should list their responses to the question or item.

2. Written Interaction   [10 minutes]

Group members place their filled-in form in the center of the table and choose one other than their own to respond to. Each person then writes comments in reaction to what the other person wrote. When finished, individuals should place the form back into the center and choose another until each person has responded to every other member of the group.

3. Analysis and Reporting   [10 minutes]

Each person reads the comments on their pads and reports them to the other members of the group. The small group summarizes their written interaction on a sheet of newsprint. An appointed member of the group reports the results back to the reconvened large group.

IDEAWRITING FROM THE PERSPECTIVE
OF THE READER AS FACILITATOR

The following is a step-by-step illustration of an Ideawriting session and how to facilitate one. In this example, Ideawriting is being used to create action plans. The group will be in the initial setting (together in one large group) only long enough for someone, probably you, to explain why the group has been convened, what they will be doing during the course of the meeting, and how the final product will be utilized. You should be prepared, just in case it is not done by someone else, to describe your role and the process that will be utilized during the meeting.

The process may be explained as follows:

In a moment, I am going to ask you to count off so that you break into groups of three and begin to develop action plans for how to achieve each of the goals that you have identified.

We are going to utilize Ideawriting to develop the action plans. The way that Ideawriting works is . . .

Using the form titled "Ideawriting Form for Action Plans," each of you write into the box called "What" the goal that you have been assigned.

Your responsibility then is to work silently and independently and fill in the remaining boxes—"How" you think the goal can be achieved by this organization, "Who" you believe should be responsible for seeing it accomplished, by "When" it should be accomplished, and "How" you will "Know" it has been accomplished. That should take you about 5 minutes.

You will then swap sheets so that each person gets someone else's ideas. Comment on what they have written down. Indicate what you like, what you don't like, and so forth. It won't take you very long to do that. Then swap again and comment on what was written down originally or what appears in the marginal comments. Keep swapping until everyone comments on everyone else's sheet.

Return the sheets to their original source, so that you can read what the others had to say about your ideas. Then carry on a conversation about what all of you seemed to like, what all of the members of the group apparently agreed on. Try, if possible, to work out any apparent differences you seem to have.

Finally, summarize what you have agreed to on a single sheet of paper and tape the sheet to the wall.

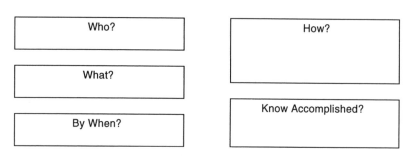

Figure 3.4. Ideawriting Form for Action Plans

Divide the group into small work groups. Your options for this include:

1. In most circumstances, simply have them count off so that they create small groups of three people (two and four are acceptable, but they should be considered the acceptable extremes). For example, if there are 10 people, have them count off up to three—that creates two groups of three and one of four. If there are 24 people, have them count off to eight which creates eight groups of 3 people. After they count off, you can assign them topics or they can be allowed, as a group, to select whichever topic they prefer.

2. Ask them to decide which item they prefer to work on. A simple way to do that is to point to the first topic (it is helpful if all of the topics are listed on a sheet of flip-chart paper), read it, and ask for a show of hands as to who wants to work on that topic. Continue on down the list, writing the number of volunteers beside each topic. With a bit of negotiation, a large group usually subdivides in a reasonable fashion. Permit groups as small as two people, but if five or more want to work on a topic, ask them to break into separate groups. For example, if six people want to work on the same topic, ask them to compose two groups of three, so that each group works independently of the other.

3. Assign people to small groups. This can be done ahead of time by giving each person a number or letter or color-coding their name badge or assignment sheet (if you use them). If your primary concern is the mix of people (e.g., you might want to be sure to mix up staff and board), you can allow each of the groups to pick their own topic. If your concern is to be certain that specific people work on specific topics, you can also assign the topic for each of the groups.

Which option you select is likely to depend on the goal for the meeting. If it is to get them working on some of their task, Options 1 or

2 are desirable. If it is necessary to get certain work accomplished, then Option 3 is probably desirable.

If, for example, the group is developing action plans for their organizational goals, there might be six goals and only enough people for four groups. If it is acceptable that work is not done on all of the goals, you have another choice, which is either to assign one of the goals to each of the groups, or to allow each group to select whichever goal they would like to work on. If the small groups only work on four of six goals, you might consider brainstorming ideas with the full group on the remaining two. The best time to do that is after they have completed their small group work on the first four.

This is the time for them to work in groups, as outlined in the process explanation above. Your only responsibilities are to:

1. Pass out the form titled "Ideawriting Form for Action Plans."

2. Make certain they write before they speak. Some people will resist writing and want to start talking right away, so you might go over to them and quietly remind them that initially they are to work silently and independently by writing down their ideas. You may want to make an announcement to the full group if a number of groups are talking.

3. Deliver a sheet of flip-chart paper and markers to each of the small groups when they begin to talk about what is on their sheets. You might bring the sheet of paper to their table or tape it on the wall near where they are working. You might even put their topic at the top of the sheet. It is also a good idea to have them put on the sheet the names of the people who worked on that topic, should you try to reconstruct something later on. It is desirable to save the marked Ideawriting forms along with the flip-chart sheets.

One way to bring closure to the session is to have a spokesperson from each small group report on the highlights of their work. A caution is to give them a very limited amount of time (one minute) or some people will bore the group with unneeded detail. On occasion, if you want more than reporting—that is, if you would like input from the full group—it may be appropriate to have a brief report from each of the small groups and to allow the full group to add ideas. Keep in mind that you may want to have the full group address topics that were not addressed by any of the small groups.

Seldom is the work done in any group an end in and of itself. An individual or a small team will have to edit the work that comes out of such an Ideawriting session.

4

Interpretive Structural Modeling

This chapter describes Interpretive Structural Modeling (ISM) and includes sections on ISM preparations, the opening statement, conducting the ISM session with a computer, and conducting the ISM session without a computer. Extended examples of ISM, with and without the computer, are included, as are sections on limitations, resources, and references. Addenda to the chapter describe coping with a large number of elements in an ISM, reviewing an ISM product, criteria for making ISM choices, and the role of a process observer. Following the addenda is an outline of ISM (called "At-a-Glance") and a detailed description of exactly what the reader could say and do if she or he were facilitating an ISM session.

Interpretive Structural Modeling (ISM) is a method of identifying and summarizing relationships among specific items that define an issue or problem. ISM provides a means by which a group can impose order on the complexity of the items. Frequently, ISM is used once a group has generated ideas through Nominal Group Technique (NGT; see Chapter 2) or Ideawriting (see Chapter 3).

As the title suggests, ISM enables a group to interpret, structure, and model its ideas. The method is interpretive in that the group's judgment decides whether and how items are related. It is structural in that, on the basis of the relationship, an overall structure is extracted from the complex set of items. It is modeling in that the specific relationships and overall structure are portrayed in graphic form.

For clarity, ISM can be broken down into four phases. The process begins with an element set composed of items relevant to an issue or problem (e.g., programs in a budget, members of an organization, factors that impede economic growth, etc.). The ISM process imposes a particular relationship between items, expressed in a phrase that leads to a paired comparison (e.g., "should be cut before," "will lead to," "is less important than," "is more important than," etc.). Next, the group is asked to compare two items (e.g., "In reducing the budget, Program A should be cut before Program B"). After discussion, the group's judgment is determined by majority vote. The vote is recorded. The group then proceeds to another comparison of two items. After all necessary comparisons have been made, a model of the group's thinking, structured by combinations of the paired comparisons, can be generated.

SUGGESTION

It is important to have a sense of how ISM works. If you are not familiar with ISM, jump ahead six pages and read "An Example Using a Computer" before you return to this point and read the remainder of the chapter.

In earlier ISM sessions, a mainframe computer was needed to expedite the process. As this chapter later explains, however, I have developed a system through which the ISM process can be managed without a computer.

CAUTION

The utilization of ISM in a group context requires a sensitivity to both its science and its art. ISM is based upon relatively complex mathematical rules. It is essential that these rules not be ignored or violated by the user. It is not critical, however, that the user completely understand the mathematical bases of the method. In fact, undue attention to the mathematic assumptions by a group leader may detract from the effectiveness of the use of ISM, especially with decision-making bodies in applied settings. An equal (or even greater) influence on the quality of results with ISM is the skill of the group leader in facilitating the group interaction. Consequently, do not overstress the mathematics of ISM, and do use the best available group process skills.

ISM PREPARATIONS

As with each of the other processes addressed in this book, there are a number of decisions to be made before a group can engage in an ISM session. It is important to allow sufficient lead time for both the technical and personnel decisions.

Technical Decisions

Item selection. As was mentioned earlier, ISM is frequently used once a group has generated ideas (i.e., items) through NGT or Ideawriting. In addition, the set of items may be fixed as in line items in a budget to be cut or a slate of candidates to be selected. When much is at stake in the results (e.g., with priority setting or budget cutting), discussion of the pairs of items can be extended and vigorous. Moreover, a particular application of ISM may require a large number of items. Therefore, consideration must be given to how long a group is willing to commit to an ISM session.

It may be necessary, due to the time available, to limit the number of items used in a session. In my judgment, most groups will be willing to consider 15 to 20 items. As you move beyond that number, the group must be prepared to expend an unusual amount of time and energy. For example, 25 items will generally require a full workday (with a computer) and 35 items, 2 full workdays.

Items to be considered during the ISM session should be of major significance to the problem at hand and carefully worded so they convey precise, clear information as briefly as possible. Nearly duplicate items should be eliminated. Less significant items should be set aside for consideration after the ISM session. Addendum 4.1 provides an illustration of one way to manage a large number of items.

Relationship phrasing. The ISM product is based on a series of group judgments regarding the relationship between two items. The relationship phrase is taken from at least one of six types of relations:

- impact
- influence
- definitive
- spatial
- temporal
- mathematical

The relationship can be expressed in a subordinate phrase, such as "is subordinate to," "reports to," "should be eliminated before," "is caused by," "helps to achieve," etc., or as a relationship denoting superiority, as in "is superior to," "supervises," "precedes," "is caused by," etc. If computer software is utilized, it likely requires the use of a subordinate phrase. In either case, the wording of the phrase must be understandable to all participants. Remember, the wording of the relationship must facilitate the comparison between items and not hinder it.

Presentational mode. A decision must be made as to how the pairs of items will be presented to the group for discussion and voting. Paired items should be presented both orally and visually. During the process, the group facilitator announces each pair. It is helpful to read the whole comparison— the two items and the relationship—for each pair. The pair can be displayed by means of an overhead projector or blackboard, a display board consisting of an easel or wall with blank spaces, or a computer terminal.

- A display screen (e.g., TV monitor, "advent" screen connected to the computer terminal). As the computer calls up item pairs, they are displayed either in full text or with identifying numbers (e.g., item 2 versus item 8).
- A display board independent of the computer. This consists of a board or an easel or wall with blank spaces before and after the phrase expressing the subordinate relation. Items are recorded on cardboard plaques so they can be hung on hooks, taped to the board, or placed on a ledge. The following is an example of one display board.

| 9. Productivity |

has a lower priority than

| 6. Flexibility |

when making decisions on funding

- An overhead projector or a blackboard could also be used in place of the screen or board.

Computer. Use of a computer may attract or inhibit potential users. The computer is attractive when people are impressed with its speed, efficiency, and neutrality. It is inhibiting when people incorrectly assume that the computer limits their discretion or control over decisions. During the ISM session, the computer simply

1. stores the items to be compared,
2. calls them up two at a time for comparison,
3. stores the results of group decisions,
4. infers certain comparisons based on previous decisions, and
5. extracts an overall structure from the perceived relationships.

The examples that follow provide the step-by-step process of the ISM with the use of a computer and without a computer, respectively.

Equipment. If a computer is used, basic equipment consists of a terminal (with a modem, if access to computer facilities that have the ISM software is required) and monitor so that the choices can be viewed by the participants. If a display screen is to be used as the mode for presenting the paired comparisons, the screen and an appropriate cable to connect the terminal to the screen must be available.

Observation charts. Observation charts for recording the group decision facilitate analysis of the session. This written backup also assures the ability to continue or recreate the ISM process in the event of a computer disruption. Figure 4.1 offers an example of a suitable observation chart.

Personnel Decisions

Although the ISM can be managed with one person, it is desirable to have at least two persons, three if using a computer. These people include the group facilitator, an observer, and a terminal operator.

The group facilitator. The person facilitating the group describes the process and the ground rules, presents the pairs of items to the group, leads the discussion so that all views are expressed, and brings the group to a vote.

An observer. The person observing the session records votes and judgments and notes significant developments occurring during the process.

The terminal operator. The person operating the computer terminal must be familiar and experienced with the ISM program—including the

CHOICES		VOTE		COMMENTS
e.g., 2 vs. 3	I	Y = yes N = no	I I	Record reasons given for voting yes or no
vs.	I	Y N	I	
vs.	I	Y N	I	
vs.	I	Y N	I	
vs.	I	Y N	I	
vs.	I	Y N	I	
vs.	I	Y N	I	

Figure 4.1. Observation Chart

software logic, program commands, and procedures. The operator is the link between the computer and the group and should be able to work effectively with both. More information dealing with using ISM with a computer is described in the following section.

OPENING STATEMENT

Briefly,

1. Stress the importance of the task.
2. Describe how the items were generated.
3. State the goal of the session.
4. Emphasize the potential usefulness of the product that will be generated.
5. Summarize the steps of the process.
6. Explain the role of the computer.

   The computer

   (a) holds the items,

   (b) calls the items up for paired comparisons,

   (c) records the results of group decisions,

   (d) infers certain comparisons based on previous decisions,

   (e) provides a structure that reflects the group's judgments.

   The computer does not

   (a) make decisions,

   (b) replace group decisions,

   (c) control the group or its decisions.

7. Present the rules of the process.

   (a) A majority vote decides.

   (b) A tie vote counts as a "no" vote (if the group is utilizing a subordinate relationship—e.g., "should be eliminated before") or a "yes" vote (if the group is utilizing a relationship denoting superiority—e.g., "is a higher priority than").

CONDUCTING THE ISM SESSION WITH A COMPUTER

The following is a procedure for considering each pair of items with the aid of a mainframe computer. This procedure is repeated for each pair until all comparisons have been made.

Step 1: Presentation of the Element Set

Facilitator	Terminal Operator	Observer
Controls which items are considered in which order and announces each pair of items as it is displayed on the screen or board. It is normally up to the facilitator to determine which new item the group will consider each time the computer is ready for one. It may be beneficial to start the process with a comparison that the group will decide on fairly easily in order to foster a climate of cooperation.	Calls up the pairs of items for comparison when asked to do so.	Notes the item pair being considered.

Step 2: Discussion Leading to Paired Comparisons

Facilitator	Terminal Operator	Observer
Leads the discussion of the item pair, making sure that all views are aired and that nonproductive conflict is contained.	Listens attentively in order to adapt the use of the computer to the needs and interests of the specific group.	Records comments on why one item is preferred over the other. It may be suitable for the observer to make observations about the group's process and progress.

Step 3: Voting

Facilitator	Terminal Operator	Observer
Brings the group to a majority rule decision on the comparison.	Types the decision into the computer and calls up the next pair of items.	Records the vote.

Step 2 is repeated until all paired comparisons have been made.

Step 4: Computer Generated Model

Shortly after the vote on the final pair of items, the computer produces the ISM structure so that it can be displayed for the participants. Figure 4.2 is an example of an ISM structure. The group should be reminded that the structure is the computer's version of the group's judgments about paired comparisons. Consequently, it may not reflect the group's judgment when the relationships among all the items are viewed as a whole. Modifications may be made in the structure and, if the participants are so inclined, they should be encouraged to make changes carefully, keeping in mind the discussion that gave rise to the original structuring.

AN EXAMPLE USING THE COMPUTER

A county board of commissioners faced difficulty in balancing its annual budget for a number of years, principally because costs rose faster than revenues. The board utilized the surpluses of previous years, reduced expenses and services, and increased revenues in order to eliminate projected budget deficits. Board members were dissatisfied with the means they had employed to make expenditure reductions and expressed the need for a more systematic, priority-oriented approach.

They decided to use an approach consisting of two steps. First, they completed a series of questionnaires to identify potential cutback units (programs or activities or program elements to be eliminated completely). Second, they participated in an ISM session to arrange the cutback units in priority order, ranging from most expendable to least expendable.

The set of items for the ISM session was produced by the questionnaires. The paired comparisons were based on the subordinate relation:

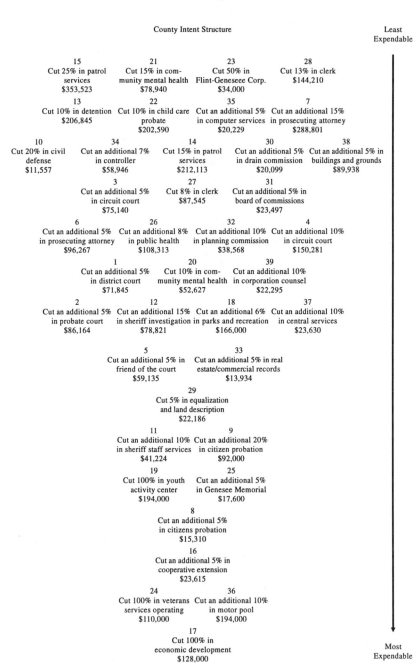

Figure 4.2. ISM Priority Structure

In reducing expenditures, should the board
of commissioners choose to cut

(item A)

---

before choosing to cut

(item B)

During the ISM session, a facilitator moderated the discussion of each paired comparison, encouraging the expression of opposing viewpoints. After everyone had an opportunity to comment, the facilitator called for a yes or no vote. Votes were stored in the computer. When all pairs of possible budget cuts had been considered, the computer provided the structure that resulted from the voting. Results were reproduced in a graphic and verbal format, like the one presented in Figure 4.1. Each item includes the number (reflecting the order in which it was considered), name, and dollar amount.

The ISM results showed the board's judgment on budget reductions. It presented a hierarchical format ranging from most expendable to least expendable. Items at the same level in the hierarchy were considered equally expendable.

The results were then studied and discussed by the board to determine if the structure produced by the paired comparisons made sense. If not, adjustments could have been made, within the limits of reasoned consideration. Addendum 4.2 provides an illustration of how one group systematically reviewed their product.

CONDUCTING THE ISM SESSION
WITHOUT A COMPUTER

The following is a procedure for considering each pair of items. This procedure is repeated for each pair until all comparisons have been made.

Step 1: Presentation of the element set

Facilitator controls which items are considered in which order. Displays two items for the group—usually 1 and 2—on the board or wall or screen. Displays the same two items—side by side—for herself or himself, usually on a table. Someone, such as an observer, may be sitting at the table and assisting by keeping track of the items.

Step 2: Discussion leading to paired comparisons

Step 3: Voting

Step 4: Group generated model

EXAMPLE

The relationship in the example is: "Is an equal or higher priority than." When the relationship is phrased such as the example, it is a relationship that claims the first item is superior. The relationship could have been phrased so that the first item was subordinate. An example of a subordinate relationship would be, "Is an equal or lower priority than." Occasionally a shorthand expression—1 R 2—is used to refer to the comparison of two items, and it means that item 1 is first, then the relationship, then item 2.

The decision-making group will see what is in the column titled "Displayed for the Group." Only the facilitator and her helper (if she has one) will see what is in the column titled "Displayed for the Facilitator." The facilitator should use 3 × 5 index cards with the number only.

Displayed for the Group	*Displayed for the Facilitator*
1. Hire a New Director	1 2

IS AN EQUAL OR HIGHER
PRIORITY THAN

2. Add a Second Secretary

If the vote is "no"—which means that the group believes that item 1 is not an equal or higher priority than item 2—the facilitator should display the outcome:

Displayed for the Group	*Displayed for the Facilitator*
	2
	1

If the vote is "yes" (to 1 R 2)—which means that the group believes that item 1 is an equal or higher priority than item 2—the facilitator should display the two items in reverse order and ask the group to discuss them and to vote again. The facilitator cannot assume that the vote means that item 1 is a higher priority than item 2. The group may believe that they are of equal priority.

Displayed for the Group	*Displayed for the Facilitator*

2. Add a Second Secretary

IS AN EQUAL OR HIGHER
PRIORITY THAN

1. Hire a New Director

If the vote is "no" (to 2 R 1), then the group has established that they believe 1 is a higher priority than 2 and the facilitator should display the outcome:

Displayed for the Group	*Displayed for the Facilitator*
	1
	2

If the group votes "yes" (to 2 R 1), which means that they have voted "yes" both ways, the group has indicated that the items are of equal value and the facilitator should display the outcome:

Displayed for the Group	*Displayed for the Facilitator*
	1 2

Assume that they voted "no" to the original choice (1 R 2), so the outcome is:

Displayed for the Group	Displayed for the Facilitator
	2
	1

The facilitator should display the next item, 3, so that it is compared with item 1.

> *HINT:* It is usually clearer to the participants if *new* items are displayed on top.

Displayed for the Group	Displayed for the Facilitator
3. Remodel Outer Office	2
IS AN EQUAL OR HIGHER PRIORITY THAN	1 3
1. Hire a New Director	

Note that the facilitator, for her own use, places the new item, 3, next to the item that it is being compared with, 1.

> *HINT:* It is desirable to place the card displayed for the facilitator so that it covers a portion of the card with which it is being compared. That way it will not be confused with items that are at the same level because they are of equal value.

If, after discussion, the group votes "no" (to 3 R 1)—which means that the group believes that 3 is not an equal or higher priority than 1, the facilitator should display the outcome:

Displayed for the Group	Displayed for the Facilitator
	2
	1
	3

There is no reason to compare 3 with 2 since the group already has established that they believe 2 is a higher priority than 1.

If the group votes "yes" (to 3 R 1) and the items are presented in reverse order (1 R 3) and the group votes "yes" again—indicating that the group believes the two items are of equal priority, the facilitator should display the outcome:

Displayed for the Group	*Displayed for the Facilitator*
	2
	1 3

If the group votes "yes" (to 3 R 1) and after the items are presented in reverse order (1 R 3) the group votes "no"—indicating that the group believes that 3 is a higher priority than 1, the group then should be asked to consider the relative priority between 3 and 2.

Displayed for the Group	*Displayed for the Facilitator*
3. Remodel Outer Office	2 3
IS AN EQUAL OR HIGHER PRIORITY THAN	1
2. Add a Second Secretary	

If, after discussion, the group votes "no" (to 3 R 2)—indicating that the group believes 2 is a higher priority than 3, the facilitator should display the outcome:

Displayed for the Group	*Displayed for the Facilitator*
	2
	3
	1

If the group votes "yes" (to 3 R 2) and the items are presented in reverse order (2 R 3) and the group votes "yes" again—indicating that the group believes the two items are of equal priority, the facilitator should display the outcome:

Displayed for the Group	Displayed for the Facilitator
	2 3
	1

If the group votes "yes" (to 3 R 2) and the items are presented in reverse order (2 R 3) and the group votes "no"—indicating that the group believes 3 is a higher priority than 2, then the facilitator should display the outcome:

Displayed for the Group	Displayed for the Facilitator
	3
	2
	1

Continue in this fashion.

Each new item can be considered in relation to any other item.

> **HINT:** A good rule of thumb is for the facilitator to begin about the middle of the structure that is displayed for the facilitator.

So, if the facilitator has something like the following:

Displayed for the Group	Displayed for the Facilitator
	2
	3
	1
	4

she should begin by considering 5 R 1 or 5 R 3. The vote will tell the facilitator whether to move up or down the structure. For example, if it is established that 5 is a higher priority than 1, 5 should be compared to 3. If it is established that 5 is a lower priority than 1, it should be compared to 4. If the group votes "yes" both ways, they have established that the two items belong on the same level. For example, if they establish that 5 and 1 are of equal priority, the structure the facilitator sees should look like:

Displayed for the Group	*Displayed for the Facilitator*
	2
	3
	1 5
	4

Remember, the group only sees the two items that the facilitator displays for them.

REVIEWING AN ISM PRODUCT

One of the strengths of ISM is that it provides the group with a way to think about the questions it has raised. The actual ISM session may be the only time spent by the group in producing the ISM model. The group may choose to accept the display as the final product because they do not have additional time to expend considering the elements or because they are satisfied with the product.

Some political situations place a premium on accepting a group product exactly as it is produced. If a limited amount of time is available for the group to deliberate or there is a conscious attempt to avoid what may be a rancorous and disruptive political climate, the group may agree at the outset that the structure that is produced will constitute the work of the group.

However, the display produced during an ISM session does not necessarily represent the final product of a group. The group members may want to review and perhaps modify the display because they are not satisfied with it or because they believe a review is in order. They may be hesitant about simply accepting one structure as the sum of all of their separate decisions. A group might review its own ISM display, have one member (or a few members) of the group review and edit the display, or ask a process observer to view the deliberation and provide a description of the display (see Addendum 4.4).

ISM is likely to be utilized initially because the group wants a systematic way to consider a set of elements. That goal of utilizing a systematic process can be undermined if the group uses a review process that is not systematic. For example, the integrity of what was produced during an ISM session would be substantially undermined if after the display was arrayed by the facilitator she said something like, "How would the group like to modify this structure?" and agreed to whatever modifications were offered by members of the group. Addendum 4.2 describes how one group systematically reviewed and modified the ISM model they had produced.

LIMITATIONS

Although the major limitation of ISM, the need for access to a mainframe computer, has been eliminated with this edition, there are still a number of potential limitations to be aware of when choosing ISM as a method of group decision making. First, special attention must be given to be certain that the items are distinct. Second, care must be taken to assure that the phrasing of the relationship elicits the desired product and is consistent throughout the exercise.

Third, of the processes addressed in this book, ISM is probably the most fatiguing for the participants. This is why it is critical that the group facilitator stress the importance of the task at hand in the opening statement.

Finally, one of the primary limitations of using ISM with a computer deals with the wording of the relationship phrase. As the underlying logic of ISM software assumes a subordinate relationship, it is critical that the subordinate phrase be used throughout the session if a computer is being used. If the group facilitator is prepared with simple examples to illustrate the group's decision-making task, adherence to this fundamental tenet will be easier.

RESOURCES

Interpretive Structural Modeling was invented by John Warfield and introduced in 1974. The most complete description can be found in Warfield (1976). A very good overview is Warfield's chapter in Olsen (1982, pp. 155-201). Those who plan to use ISM should be acquainted with Warfield's work.

ADDENDUM 4.1
COPING WITH A LARGE NUMBER
OF ELEMENTS IN AN ISM

This addendum describes how to cope with a large number of elements in an ISM session.

It takes a substantial amount of time for a group to consider a large number of elements during an ISM session. If a group is properly prepared and committed to producing a useful product, they are normally willing to expend the time. But if they are not adequately prepared, are reluctant participants, or do not have much time, they may react negatively to the amount of time it takes and to the necessary repetition of items.

This addendum describes two examples in which I tried an innovation to enable a group to structure a large number of items by considering a small subset of items. The first example concerns a budget reduction process with a county government. The second example, also involving a county government, describes a group's attempt to prioritize a large number of potential work statements. In addition to illustrating how a group might manage the complexity of a large number of elements, both examples demonstrate how processes are linked together in order to achieve a goal defined by a group.

A Budget Reduction Process

A county government had an anticipated shortfall of $3.6 million between the requested budget and anticipated revenues, approximately 7% of the total budget. The commissioners were not looking forward to making tough decisions about budget reductions because they had done that the previous year and the experience was frustrating. They had avoided making some decisions the previous year by drawing down on (using) reserve money. Reserve money was were no longer available. The controller thought the board would benefit by participating in focused deliberations. The commissioners had used a focused process a few years earlier and were pleased with the outcome. After the decision was made to initiate a process, these steps were followed:

1. Budget information was requested from the controller's office (by the consultants responsible for conducting the process). The budget information was reviewed and additional information was requested.

2. A questionnaire was prepared that listed each of the components that could be considered for reduction, provided essential information about each component, and asked the commissioners to designate the most desired level of funding (by an X) and the minimum acceptable level of funding (by a Z) for each component. Figure A4.1 is a sample of three of the items in the questionnaire. The general budget category is "Equalization and Land Description," and the first specific budget component (three components are included in Figure A4.1) is "Record Development—Master Tax Files." The number one (1) within the parentheses indicates that it is category one, which designates a discretionary service. Also included is the actual budget utilized in 1982 ($179,916) and the proposed budget for 1983 ($193,507). The scale reflects the percentages and actual dollar amounts that would be reflected at each percentage level. The commissioners, who were the respondents, were asked to mark an X at the spot on the scale they thought was the most desirable level of funding and a Z at the spot they thought was the minimum acceptable level of funding. The scale ranges from 0% to 120%, because it was not possible to indicate that a program should get less than zero dollars but it was possible to designate that a program should get more than 100% of what they requested. If, for example, the most desirable level of funding was 90% of the amount requested, that would be $174,156.

3. The questionnaires were distributed and explained to the board.

4. Budget hearings were conducted the following week in order to give the commissioners an opportunity to request whatever information they required in order to complete the questionnaires.

5. The questionnaires were independently completed and returned.

6. The questionnaires were analyzed. Two reports were prepared that (a) arrayed the board's collective responses for each budget component (Figure A4.2 is a sample of the first report) and (b) described the implications of their decisions for the budget. Figure A4.2 indicates that on item "14. Real Estate Records," the largest group of respondents (6) indicated that the most desirable level of funding was 95%. Two people marked 90% and one marked 75%.

7. Interpretive Structural Modeling was utilized to determine the priority for 23 budget components. A meeting was held with the board that reviewed the steps that had already been taken and had them participate in an ISM session.

MANAGEMENT AND PLANNING

Equalization and Land Description

1. Record Development - Master Tax Files (1, 1982: $179,916; 1983: $193,507)

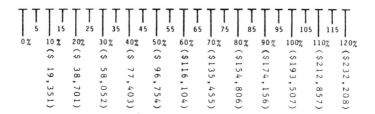

2. Valuation Analysis - Equalization (1, 1982: $379,686; 1983: $384,704)

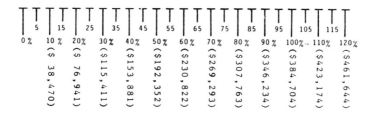

Revenue Management

3. Treasurer Accomodation Tax (1, 1982: $696,427; 1983: $709,935) - $3,600 has been subtracted from 1983 request

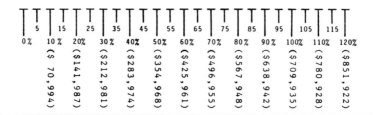

Figure A4.1. Sample of Questionnaire

14. Real Estate Records			15. Land-Use Transportation		
	Most desirable	Minimum acceptable		Most desirable	Minimum acceptable
100	XXXXX		100	XXX	
95	XXXXXX	ZZZZ	95	XXXXXX	ZZ
90	XX	ZZZZZ	90	XX	ZZZZZ
85		ZZ	85		Z
80			80	X	Z
75	X	Z	75		ZZ
70			70		
65			65		
60			60		
55			55		
50		Z	50		
45			45		
40			40		
35			35		
30			30		
25			25		
20			20		
15			15		
10			10		
5			5		
0			0	XX	Z

Figure A4.2. Sample of Board's Responses

The original intent was to conduct the ISM over approximately $1\frac{1}{2}$ days. The expectation was that between 30 and 40 items would be considered during the course of the ISM session. The reason for that number was that approximately that number of items were considered during the previous process 3 years earlier.

In order to keep the items as comparable as possible, only budget components greater than $300,000 were considered for potential cuts. This number was used as the demarcation because it provided about the right number of items. Once the arbitrary decision was made to use that number, the list of items above that amount was carefully examined in order to be certain that there would be a diversity of items in terms of the percentage size of the cuts, and that potential cuts were included from each of the sections of the budget. All of the components could not be considered in the ISM, so it was necessary to deliberate over a range of items that were both diverse and representative. The goal was to produce an ISM product that was representative of the whole budget.

Once the ISM was under way, it became apparent that the commissioners' interactions were not as energetic or as well informed as they were when the process had been used earlier with the previous board. Attendance during the course of the ISM session was sporadic, and many of the commissioners had not set aside sufficient time to work late that evening. It was decided that a concerted effort would be made to have the board consider items from each segment of the budget, but that whatever the board finished the first day would provide the basis for their initial priority structure. In all, 23 items were considered by the commissioners.

8. The following morning, a questionnaire was prepared that included the "first priority structure" (the 23 budget components) and asked the commissioners to "assign a number to each of the 60 [remaining] items to reflect your estimate of its priority" in light of the priority given to the 23 items constituting the first priority structure.

9. Questionnaires were distributed and explained to the board at 11:00 a.m. that same day.

10. The questionnaires were independently completed and returned within 30 minutes of their distribution.

11. The questionnaire responses were tabulated and a value was given to each budget component.

12. All budget components were arrayed in one priority structure.

13. The priority structure was presented to the board at 2:00 p.m. that day. It was explained that if a line were drawn at a certain point and if the board made the recommended cuts below that line, they would reach their deficit and would not have to make any of the cuts in the budget components above the line. The spirit of the discussion following the presentation of the priority structure was that if commissioners wanted to preserve items below the line, they would have to develop rational and fair ways to trade off with items above the line.

It would not have been possible to conduct the ISM with all 83 potential budget reductions. Nevertheless, the intention was to conduct the ISM with more than the 23 that were eventually considered. Situational factors dictated the number that was considered.

It seems reasonable to conduct the ISM with fewer than the maximum number of items, so long as there are good reasons for the items that are considered. It is difficult for some groups to sustain their attention long enough to consider a large number of items. The first time ISM was used with the county board, it took them 1½ days to consider 33 items. If fewer items are considered, it is more likely that such a budget reduction process can fit into busy schedules and the debate over items may be improved because the participants do not get fatigued. Another difference between the first time the process was used with the board and this instance is that this time it was possible to produce a priority structure that included all of the budget components. Creating a partial framework (with 23 items) and then using a questionnaire to fit all of the remaining 60 items into the framework did allow the board to prioritize all of the potential budget cuts.

A Priority-Setting Process

A county administrator directed all department heads to prepare work statements identifying major efforts. These were not to be statements of the obvious day-to-day activities but work efforts "over and above." For example, pumping 40 million gallons of water per day was considered routine. Combining city and county water supplies was considered over and above. Disposing of 1,000 tons of garbage a day—routine; installing electrostatic precipitators—over and above. Implementing an accrual accounting system, developing an energy conservation program, getting voter approval on a new concept for financing human services, and contracting for a new telephone system are a few additional examples of over and above.

After a new commissioner took office, it was decided that it was an appropriate time to educate and orient the new commissioner to the county's activities, as well as to prioritize, all at one time, the prospective work activities that were over and above, beyond the routine functioning of the county government. Interpretive Structural Modeling was selected as the essential process to determine the priority of county work activities, expressed as "work statements."

The Process

A series of steps was followed in order to identify the relative priority of the proposed work statements. First, work statements were drafted by department heads. The statements were reviewed and some were rewritten (by the department head) to make certain they were clear and simple and identified the specific outcome that would result if the work was undertaken by the county.

Second, in order to present the commission with work statements that were different from those generated by each of the departments (in the words of the county administrator, "to allow them to dream a little"), the county executive staff used NGT to identify additional potential work statements. They were asked, "If resources were not an issue and if you were a county commissioner, what is it you would have the county doing?" The 9 highest rated activities were selected from the 30 the executive staff identified.

A questionnaire was prepared and sent to the commissioners. The questionnaire included the department work statements and the items identified by the executive staff. If a justification was provided by the department head, it was included as a parenthetical statement immediately following the work statement. The commissioners were asked to judge whether each of the statements was clear and what was the priority (high, moderate, low, or no priority) of each of the statements. Space was provided for the commissioners to identify activities that were not included in the questionnaire but that they believed ought to be undertaken.

A training session was provided for one of the county staff and one of the commissioners to introduce them to ISM.

The highlight of the process was a full day retreat to establish the priorities of the work statements. The county administrator explained the need for setting priorities. He commended the county's management personnel for their efforts in handling a large number of work programs and handling them well. The fact that this was being accomplished with a limited bureaucracy was cited as all the more reason why priority setting was necessary. He framed the exercise by stating, "With all there is to do, what would you have us do if we could accomplish only a dozen work programs this year?" Then the commissioners participated in an ISM session during which they structured the relationships among 19 of the work statements.

The limited time available (one day) did not allow the commissioners to consider all 115 work statements. Therefore, 19 of the 115 were selected according to the following criteria. At least one item was selected from each of the nine departments/categories. If there was a choice between general items with a policy implication and more specific items, a preference was given to the more general items. An effort was made to include those items where the responses to the questionnaire indicated that there were differences in perceived priority among the commissioners. Also, an effort was made to select items that reflected the range of the commissioners' priorities. All of the items ranged from 1.00 (high priority) to 3.00 (low priority), so approximately

40% of the items (7 to 8) were from category 1.00, another 40% from categories 1.66 through 2.33, and the remaining 20% (2 to 4) from categories 2.66 through 3.00.

Eighteen items were originally selected as the number for the ISM session because it was thought that was as large a number as the commissioners could consider in the time available. A 19th item was added because it was suggested by one of the commissioners in response to the questionnaire.

The commissioners compared each of the 19 work statements by means of paired comparisons. The same relationship was used for all comparisons. The following is an example:

IT IS A HIGHER PRIORITY TO

1. Employ a licensed long-term care administrator
as a permanent superintendent of the County Home

THAN IT IS TO

2. Perform a professional countywide human services
needs assessment.

A computer program was used to store the decisions and to provide direction to the group regarding which comparisons needed to be made. It took the commissioners approximately $3\frac{1}{4}$ hours (with an interruption for lunch) to complete the ISM. They made 98 decisions, rather than the 285 that would have been necessary if they had considered every possible comparison. They did not have to make every comparison because of the logic built into the computer software.

Within a few minutes of their last vote, the commissioners were presented with a second questionnaire that arrayed the priority structure for 19 work statements. They actually considered 18, rather than 19, work statements as one was dropped from consideration during the course of the deliberations.

They were then asked to put the remaining 96 work statements into priority order. They were instructed to use the priority structure they had created during the ISM as a framework and, in light of that framework, to assign a number to each of the items that reflected their estimate of its priority. It was explained that:

> If a component has the same priority as the items at one of the levels (e.g., level 3), give it the number of that level (in this case that would be a 3).

If a component has priority somewhere between two levels (e.g., between levels 3 and 4), give it the appropriate midpoint designation (in this case that would be a 3.5).

It took the three commissioners approximately 20 minutes to independently select an appropriate level for the remaining 96 work statements. The commissioners' responses were tabulated. It was assumed that it would be misleading to use the arithmetic mean (the average) of the three scores, because if one commissioner varied significantly from the other two, the product would not represent the preference of the majority. Therefore, the median (the midpoint) score was utilized. This decision protected the preference of the majority but did not make a substantial difference, as a test of the similarities between the commissioners' scores revealed that there was such a high agreement among the three commissioners, the similarity could not have occurred by chance.

The 96 remaining work statements were placed into the priority structure created by the original 18 work statements, and the board was presented with a 15-level priority structure that included all 114 work statements (see Figure A4.3).

While the commissioners' questionnaires were being tabulated, James Kunde, executive director of the Public Services Institute, discussed with them his reactions to their deliberations during the course of the ISM session. Addendum 4.4, "The Role of a Process Observer," is a written version of his remarks. One conclusion that Kunde shared with the commissioners at the retreat was that they dealt with more policy issues in one day than any other community had ever done. The group adjourned after a brief discussion of how the priority structure might be utilized by the commission and the county executive staff.

Results

This experiment demonstrated that a large number of elements could be managed by first considering a subset of the elements and then by placing the remaining elements into the structure that was created. Other results concern the operations of the county.

Was it useful to conduct the ISM session and to place all potential work statements into a priority structure? First of all, the exercise provided the commissioners with an opportunity to deliberate on the importance of selected county work activities away from the routine of day-to-day business. Moreover, as the executive staff was present, they

Level 1: (HIGHEST PRIORITY)

CA4 CA5 HS1 OMB1 OMB2 OMB3 OMB6 OMB9 OMB11 PR6 PR24 PD3 PD7 SE5 SE21

Level 2:

CA2 AS4 OMB4 OMB7 OMB8 OMB12 OMB13 PR1 PR2 PD1 PD4 PD5 PD6 SE1 SE10 SE11 SE22 ES6 ES8 ES9

Level 2.5:

PR22

Level 3:

CA3 CA7 AS2 CED2 CED3 HS3 OMB5 OMB10 PR4 PR7 PR23 PD2 SE2 SE6 SE7 SE24 ES7

Level 3.5:

PR21

Level 4:

AS1 AS3 CED9 HS4 HS8 PR5 PR8 PR11 PR15 PR16 PR17 SE18 SE23 SE26 SE27 SE31 ES2 NEW ITEM

Level 4.5:

PR9

Level 5:

AS5 AS6 AS7 CED1 CED7 CED8 HS5 HS6 HS7 PR3 PR19 PR20 SE8 SE9 SE20 SE28

Level 6:

PR10 PR13 SE4 SE14 SE30 ES4 ES5

Level 7:

CA6 CED4 HS2 SE13 SE15 SE16 SE17 SE19

Level 8:

CED5 PR12 SE3 SE12 SE25

Level 9:

ES1

Level 10:

SE29 ES3

Level 11:

CED6

Level 12: (LOWEST PRIORITY)

PR 14

Figure A4.3. ISM-Related Priority Structure

clarified the meaning of certain activities and learned more about specific county operations.

Second, the commission produced a different structure of priorities than they had produced without the benefit of the paired comparisons and the interchange of facts and values. For example, two thirds of the

18 work statements that constituted the ISM deliberations ended up at a different level in the ISM-related priority structure than they were after the priority rankings given them in the first questionnaire. Some were found to have a higher priority, and others were found to be of a lower priority, but the important point is that the priority was different after the commissioners had an opportunity to inform one another, ask questions of the county staff, and deliberate on the relative priority of each of the items.

Approximately one week after the retreat, the executive staff reflected on the process and concluded that the process informed them regarding how the commissioners felt about issues and programs. They enjoyed the session, in part because it was not intimidating. At least one department was going to explore different ways of accomplishing their work statements in light of the feedback from the commissioners. They suggested that the ISM process could be used to get all elected officials to talk to one another and that a similar approach should be considered for budget-cutting purposes. The executive staff observed that, to avoid any confusion in using the process in the future, the work statements needed to focus on outcomes (what would be accomplished) rather than on processes (what the department would do).

An examination of the items by department revealed that the items within two departments were consistently given the highest priority: Office of Management and Budget and the Personnel Department. Any number of interpretations can be placed on that observation: The commissioners are concerned with efficiency and these are the two departments that can generate more efficient operations, these items are doable (can be accomplished at this time), it is the right time to address these items, these are the departments in which there is the greatest need for reform, or, in the words of one of the members of the executive staff, "If you want an item to get a high score, neglect to do it; if you maintain the system, you will get a low score."

The county administrator reflected on the process:

> You might say that all of the work programs will be done eventually. So why rank them? Maybe your organizations can afford enough staff to do everything, but most cannot. Besides, it was shown that items believed to be top priority were in fact not and that policy directions were sometimes totally misunderstood by staff. The entire exercise was enlightening to all. Even though we didn't end up identifying a dozen things to do "come heck or high water," we did develop a worthwhile, useful list of priorities referred to frequently by the Commission and staff.

In their year-end report, the county commissioners specifically identified the priority-setting exercise as one of the most important accomplishments of the year.

NOTE

The example used to illustrate ISM in Chapter 4 was also of a budget reduction process in a county government. It was the same county 3 years earlier. The example in Addendum 4.1 illustrates an attempt to improve on the first application. Two significant features of the second application were (a) having the county commissioners deliberate over a smaller number of elements during the ISM session and (b) producing a priority structure of all of the potential budget reductions.

ADDENDUM 4.2
REVIEWING AN ISM PRODUCT

This addendum describes how a group systematically reviewed the product of an ISM session.

After a group uses Interpretive Structural Modeling to produce a product, they may want to accept or to review the product that has been produced. Examples of an ISM product would be a priority structure (Figure 4.1 is an example of such a structure) or an intent structure that illustrates the relationship between a set of items. This addendum describes the creation and refinement of an intent structure.

One of the strengths of ISM is that it provides a group a way to think about the question it has raised. The actual ISM session, during which the group makes paired comparisons and then gets a display of the structure (created by the way they voted on the comparisons), may be the only time spent by the group in producing the product. The group may choose to accept the display as the final product because they do not have additional time to expend considering the elements or because they are satisfied with the product.

Some political situations place a premium on accepting a group product exactly as it is produced. If a limited amount of time is available for the group to deliberate or there is a conscious attempt to avoid what may be a rancorous and disruptive political climate, the group may agree at the outset that the structure that is produced will constitute the work of the group.

However, the display produced during an ISM session does not necessarily represent the final product of a group. The group members may want to review and perhaps modify the display because they are not satisfied with it or because they believe a review is in order. They may be hesitant about simply accepting one structure as the sum of all of their separate decisions.

A group might review its own ISM display, have one member (or a few members) of the group review and edit the display, or ask a process observer to view the deliberations and provide a description of the display (see Addendum 4.4).

ISM is likely to be utilized initially because the group wants a systematic way to consider a set of elements. That goal—of utilizing a systematic process—can be undermined if the group uses a review process that is not systematic. For example, the integrity of what was produced during an ISM session would be substantially undermined if, after the display was arrayed by the facilitator, he or she said something like, "How would the group like to modify this structure?" and agreed to whatever modifications were offered by members of the group. The remainder of this chapter describes how one group systematically reviewed an ISM product they produced.

Using ISM in Strategic Planning

A county secured a grant from the federal Department of Housing and Urban Development in order to plan how the public and private sectors could work together to provide better planning for the county. Active participation by a group of citizens, the county executive staff, and the county commissioners resulted in long-range goals, objectives, and strategies in three major areas of county government.

Various group process techniques were utilized in order to enable the diverse group to contribute productively to the project. For example, 45 community leaders participated in a "nominal group conference" in which they collectively identified 153 issues, problems, and opportunities that the county should address to make it "a better place to live in the 1980s." A follow-up questionnaire was used to determine the priority of the items and whether the county had a direct, indirect, or no role in addressing each issue. A group of public officials and subject-matter experts participated in a process to determine the relationships among the issues that the respondents ranked high in importance. This step—to determine the relationship among the high-priority issues—is the focus of this addendum.

The relation used in the ISM was "help achieve." In making the paired comparisons, therefore, the group voted on questions like the following:

In improving public services in the county, will . . .
18. Expansion and Support of Preventive Health Care Programs

help achieve . . .
14. Provisions of Adequate Health Services for the Elderly?

Figure A4.2:1 is the structure that was produced by the group. Note that you read from right to left, so that item 3 helps to achieve items 9 and 19, item 9 helps to achieve items 7, 8, and 10, and so forth.

ISM Structure

The ISM structure displayed below was produced in response to the question: "In improving public services in Montgomery County, will: item ___ help achieve item ___?" Therefore, read from right to left below. For example, item 3 helps to achieve items 9 and 19. Item 9 helps to achieve items 8, 7, and 10. And so forth.

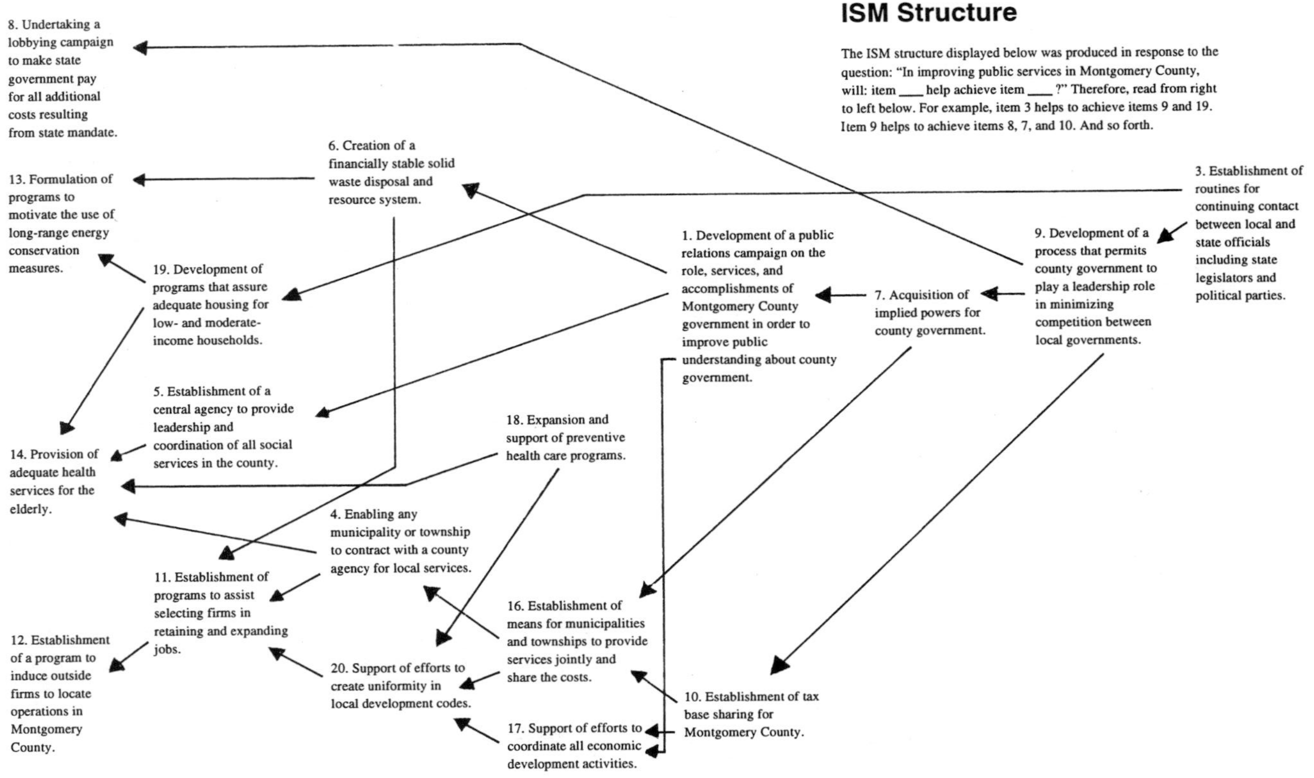

Figure A4.2:1. Original ISM Structure

A decision was made to review the structure, and the group met again about a month later for that purpose. The procedures described below were followed so the review would be systematic. The reader will recognize the essential technique as a variation of Ideawriting (see Chapter 3).

1. The initial structure (Figure A4.2:1) was presented and discussed. Copies of the structure were distributed to the group and a large version of it on newsprint (approximately 6 feet by 14 feet) was taped to the wall.

2. The 15 participants were divided into smaller groups of 3 or 4 persons. Each group was situated around a small table, approximately the size of a card table.

3. Each of the small groups was given three different sets of ISM response sheets. Figure A4.2:2 is an example of one sheet. In designing the sheet, the assumption was made that it would be desirable to examine the initial structure (Figure A4.2:1) by focusing on the items that were related. Figure A4.2:2 is just one of many sheets that were prepared for the session, and it focuses on which items are related to item 13.

4. The members of the small groups independently completed the ISM response sheets. This was very much like the initial response step in Ideawriting.

5. The small groups discussed similarities and differences in how they completed the ISM response sheets. For example, after the members in the group considering the sheet in Figure A4.2:2 completed their individual, independent reactions, the group discussed the similarities and differences on their sheets. The purpose of this step was to stimulate their thinking about the relationship between the items and, if possible, to come to a group view of the items.

6. Each of the small groups reported to the full group.

7. The full group reacted to the reports of the small groups. The group discussed whether the items in the initial structure (Figure A4.2:1) were phrased correctly, were related (e.g., whether an arrow really should go from 6 to 13), and whether or not there might be items that should be added to the structure.

This discussion resulted in changes to the initial structure (Figure A4.2:1). Figure A4.2:3 reflects the modifications that were made as a result of reviewing the initial structure.

A comparison of Figures A4.2:3 and A4.2:1 reveals that a variety of changes were made in the initial structure. There were changes in the

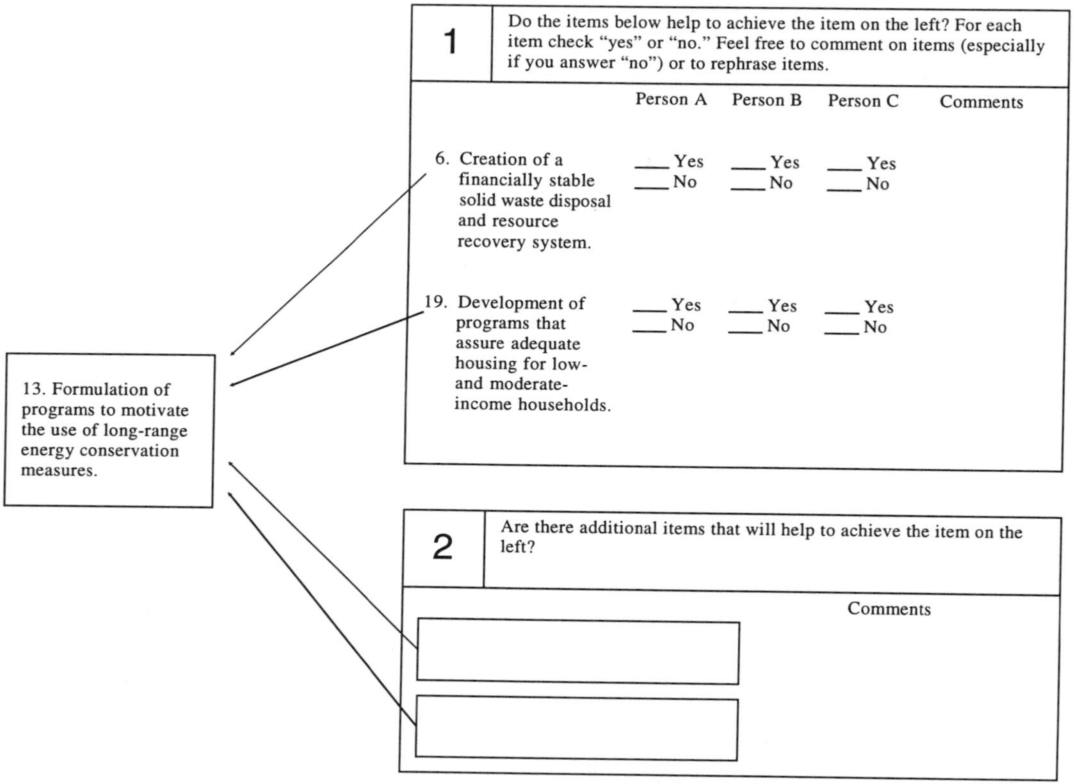
1
Do the items below help to achieve the item on the left? For each item check "yes" or "no." Feel free to comment on items (especially if you answer "no") or to rephrase items.
Person A
Person B
Person C
Comments
6. Creation of a financially stable solid waste disposal and resource recovery system.
___ Yes ___ No
___ Yes ___ No
___ Yes ___ No
19. Development of programs that assure adequate housing for low- and moderate-income households.
___ Yes ___ No
___ Yes ___ No
___ Yes ___ No
13. Formulation of programs to motivate the use of long-range energy conservation measures.
2
Are there additional items that will help to achieve the item on the left?
Comments

Figure A4.2:2. ISM Response Sheet

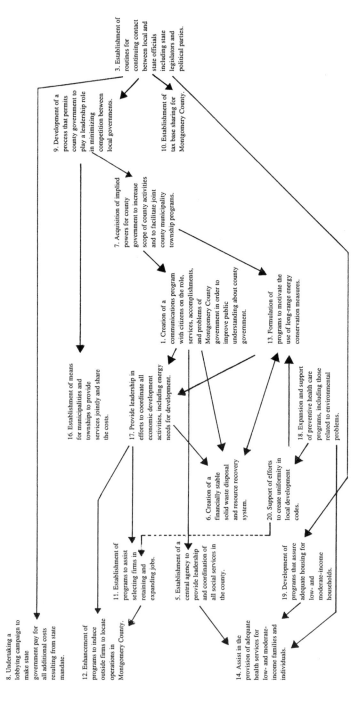

Revised ISM Structure

The ISM structure displayed below was produced by reviewing and refining the original ISM structure. Read from right to left. For example, item 3 helps to achieve items 8, 9, 10, and 19. And so forth.

3. Establishment of routines for continuing contact between local and state officials including state legislators and political parties.

9. Development of a process that permits county government to play a leadership role in minimizing competition between local governments.

10. Establishment of tax base sharing for Montgomery County.

7. Acquisition of implied powers for county government to increase scope of county activities and to facilitate joint county municipality township programs.

1. Creation of a communications program with citizens on the role, services, accomplishments, and problems of Montgomery County government in order to improve public understanding about county government.

13. Formulation of programs to motivate the use of long-range energy conservation measures.

16. Establishment of means for municipalities and townships to provide services jointly and share the costs.

17. Provide leadership in efforts to coordinate all economic development activities, including energy needs for development.

18. Expansion and support of preventive health care programs, including those related to environmental problems.

8. Undertaking a lobbying campaign to make state government pay for all additional costs resulting from state mandate.

12. Enhancement of programs to induce outside firms to locate operations in Montgomery County.

11. Establishment of programs to assist selecting firms in retaining and expanding jobs.

5. Establishment of a central agency to provide leadership and coordination of all social services in the county.

6. Creation of a financially stable solid waste disposal and resource recovery system.

20. Support of efforts to create uniformity in local development codes.

14. Assist in the provision of adequate health services for low- and moderate-income families and individuals.

19. Development of programs that assure adequate housing for low- and moderate-income households.

Figure A4.2.3. Revised ISM Structure

phrasing of five of the items. For example, item 7 in the initial structure was:

7. Acquisition of implied powers for county government.

It became:

7. Acquisition of implied powers for county government to increase scope of county activities and to facilitate joint county-municipality-township programs.

Item 14 in the initial structure was:

14. Provision of adequate health services for the elderly.

It became:

14. Assist in the provision of adequate health services for low- and moderate-income families and individuals.

Two items (10 and 13) were placed differently in the structure. There were changes in how items were related. New relations were added. In the revised structure,

- item 3 will help to achieve items 8 and 10,
- item 9 will help to achieve item 16,
- item 7 will help to achieve item 13, and
- item 17 will help to achieve items 6, 11, and 12.

Previous relations were deleted. In the revised structure,

- item 9 will not help to achieve items 8 or 10,
- item 7 will not help to achieve item 16,
- item 10 will not help to achieve items 16 or 17,
- item 16 will not help to achieve items 4 or 20,
- item 17 will not help to achieve item 20,
- item 6 will not help to achieve item 11, and
- item 19 will not help to achieve item 13.

Two items (11 and 20) were related by dotted, rather than by solid, lines, suggesting that they were indirectly—rather than directly—related.

The arrow between 6 and 13 goes in both directions. The arrow between 20 and 13 goes only to the right. There was one deletion, item 4. It is apparent that the changes in how items were related are at least in part due to the changes in the phrasing and placement of items. The members of the group agreed that the revised structure was an improvement on the initial structure.

Summary

This addendum describes how one group systematically reviewed an ISM product that they produced. It was assumed that it would not be adequate for the group simply to begin talking about the initial structure they produced. Instead,

- the initial structure was presented and discussed;
- the participants were divided into small groups;
- the small groups, using ISM response sheets, reviewed related components of the initial structure;
- the small groups reported to the full group; and
- the full group reacted to the reports of the small groups.

The result was that substantial and seemingly beneficial changes were made in the initial structure. The revised structure provided guidance for the remainder of the strategic planning process. Participants working on different components of the planning process could use the revised structure to understand the interrelationships between various aspects of the plan. Once produced, the strategic plan was used by the county to provide policy guidelines for decisions that had to be made by various departments as well as the Board of County Commissioners.

The tentative lessons about group process suggested by this one application are that it is desirable for a review of an ISM product to be focused, that Ideawriting is a technique that can be used for this purpose, and that a systematic review of an ISM product is likely to produce beneficial changes in an initial structure.

ADDENDUM 4.3
CRITERIA FOR MAKING CHOICES

This addendum identifies criteria that a group can utilize to help them select among ideas.

One of the benefits to a group using ISM to select among ideas is that it provides an opportunity to agree on what their shared criteria or values are. One way to learn about the group's shared values is for someone to listen to them deliberate and then reflect out loud before the group what they heard. "Addendum 4.4: The Role of a Process Observer" illustrates that method. In contrast to that approach, it is possible, and often desirable, for the group to deliberate on criteria (values) before they begin to use the ISM process to establish an order between a set of elements.

On a number of occasions I have assisted organizations and groups of organizations to establish the relative priority of perceived needs within their community. In each instance they asked for assistance because they believed that if there was an agreed-to list of such priorities they could make better decisions about the allocation of scarce resources. Based primarily on that work—helping people to establish the relative priority of perceived needs—the following set of potential criteria were created.

"Discuss It"
Decision-Making Criteria

D	Doable	Can it be done? In a timely fashion?
I	Impact	Impact on other (needs? activities?—whatever the nature of the items in the element set is)
S	Sequence	Should it be done before other items?
C	Capacity	Resources currently within the status quo?
U	Uniqueness	A new contribution?
S	Scope	Number affected?
S	Severity	Is a serious problem addressed?
I	Interest	Fit with organization's mission, interests?
T	Turf	Others in the same business?

What I have learned is that if I ask people, before they begin comparing needs, "What are the criteria that you are likely to use to determine whether one need has a higher priority than another?" I draw a blank. Most people are not aware of criteria in the abstract. Therefore, to have a useful discussion about criteria, it is important to "prime the pump," to provide potential criteria to select among.

If time permits, it is useful to conduct an ISM on the criteria using the relationship, "Is an equal or higher priority than." That serves two benefits. First, it enables the group to establish the relative priority of the criteria, which they can refer to when they are comparing needs. That gives the group some confidence that they are assessing each of the needs in the same way. It is important for a group to believe they are making consistent decisions, because if they do not believe that, it can undermine confidence in their work. If the group does not discuss criteria before starting, or if they do not reach some agreement on which criteria are most important, then someone who does not like the way decisions are being made is likely to accuse the group of being inconsistent.

A second benefit of using ISM to establish the relative priority of the criteria is that it helps the group to learn the process that they will be utilizing once they begin the comparison of the elements—in this case, the needs. There is always a bit of a learning curve with an ISM. So if the group uses ISM on the criteria, they are familiar with the process when they turn to the comparison of the needs. This counters a reoccurring problem; some people may believe they did not make the right decisions when they considered the first few items because they really had not caught on to the process yet.

The "Discuss It" criteria are potentially useful whenever a group is setting priorities for needs or actions. With some modification, they have been used to begin discussions of criteria for other applications of ISM, such as candidates for budget reduction.

ADDENDUM 4.4
THE ROLE OF A PROCESS OBSERVER

JAMES KUNDE

This addendum describes the role of a process observer in an ISM session.

Chapter 4 explains that a person observing an ISM session can record votes and judgments, as well as note significant developments occurring during the process. James Kunde, executive director of the Public Services Institute, played the role of a process observer in the county priority-setting project described in Addendum 4.1. Another person was responsible for recording the votes and the reasons given by the commissioners for their preferences, allowing Kunde to focus on other aspects of the deliberations.

His goal was to identify the criteria that the commissioners appeared to be using in order to determine why one potential project would have priority over another. The reason for trying to ascertain the criteria was the assumption that such information could be used by the commissioners to make future decisions. Earlier attempts to get groups to identify their decision-making criteria, apart from actually making the decisions, produced products that were suspect. It appeared to me and to Kunde that when political groups such as elected officials decide on criteria in the abstract, they produce what they think people expect of them, rather than what actually motivates their decision making. Hence, this was an attempt to identify criteria that were used by the commissioners as they made choices between potential work activities.

A REFLECTIVE ANALYSIS OF
DECISION CRITERIA AND GROUP VALUES

by James Kunde
Executive Director, Public Services Institute

It is a generally accepted principle in decision-making theory that values guide decision criteria and criteria guide a rational decision process. In practice, however, elected official bodies seldom articulate values and form decision criteria that they use in decision making. In fact, when decision-making criteria are explicitly formulated, they are often not consonant with the applied values of the group and are not adhered to in practice.

The use of the computer-assisted process of Interpretive Structural Modeling in elected body decision making has provided a rational structure for public decision making. The Commission utilized this process to rank 18 items that provided the structure for ultimately ranking 115 items in priority order for the 1983 budget year.

As the decision process proceeded, notes were taken as items were discussed and then voted on. As each decision was made, the primary decision criterion that "seemed" to be used was noted as well as any secondary criterion—especially where a controversial discussion pitted one criterion against another. The most frequently noted criteria were then compared against the structure of the 19 items originally ranked and examined for consistency. The results were then shared with the Commissioners at the end of the exercise to test whether the criteria seemed realistic to them when viewed as a whole.

As a result, of this process, the following decision criteria seemed to have been implicitly used:

1. *Timeliness and sequence.* Out of a number of important things to do, the most important criterion seems to be, "Is it the right time to tackle this job and/or is it the right next step in a sequence?"

2. *Efficiency.* Efficiency was not always the winning criterion, but it was the most important when the credibility of the Commission was in doubt or when there were too few items to show an image of efficiency in government. This suggests that an "efficient image" is very important.

3. *Doability.* This is a practicability test. "Can we really do this item, or will we end up looking silly for saying we'll do something we really can't accomplish?"

4. *Coordinator role.* The Commission was concerned that they were the highest local governmental level in the metropolitan area; therefore, they needed to demonstrate a coordinator role among lower level government to fulfill the image of being a successful institution.

5. *Consistency.* This was a frequently mentioned criterion that often lost out to timeliness or efficiency, but that held considerable importance when other criteria did not overwhelm it. "How does this fit with what we've done before and established as a pattern of action?"

6. *Protecting the public from overprofessionalization.* This criterion generally lost out to efficiency when the image of an effective

county government was involved, but it repeatedly asserted itself in the human services area.

7. *Balance.* Whenever priority concerns began accumulating in one organizational division or weren't developing in another division, Commissioners became concerned that some areas of their operation might feel less valued than others. While this did not directly upset the other higher criteria, it frequently entered into the conversation as a comment aimed at an administrator whose program just lost out to another.

8. *Longer range impact.* This was clearly not a dominant criterion, but it did enter into the conversation fairly frequently. While it usually lost out to other criteria, it was important enough to bring up.

Values

If one arranges the above criteria in their apparent relative order of priority, it looks approximately as follows:

Timeliness
Sequence
Efficiency   Doability
Coordinator Role
Consistency
Protection from
Overprofessionalization
Balance
Long Range

This suggests that the primary values of the Commissioners relative to county government might be:

- Responsive—about how to deliver timely, good services
- Holistic—broad in outlook and overview
- Humane and client oriented
- Structurally balanced with capable people throughout the system

It might be interesting to see if future administrative reports to the Commission are better received if they address the above values and criteria. If so, the exercise suggests that it might truly be better to develop decision criteria *after* an exercise of rational decision making, as opposed to before.

ISM-AT-A-GLANCE

Meeting Preparation

- Select items to be compared.
- Determine relationship that will be used to make the comparisons.
- Decide on a way to array the items (overhead projector, blackboard, display board, computer terminal).
- Establish what roles participants in the process will play (facilitator, observer, terminal operator—if a computer is being utilized).
- Prepare the meeting room.
- Assemble equipment (overhead projector, computer terminal) and supplies (markers, chalk, index cards, placards or paper).
- If using a display board, prepare placards or sheets of paper with the items being compared, numbering the items.
- Create a set of 3 × 5 cards with numbers on them.

Opening Statement

Stress the importance of the task. Explain how items were generated. State the goal of the session. Emphasize potential usefulness of the product that will be generated. Summarize the steps of the ISM process. If using a computer, explain its role. Present the rules of the process.

Conducting the ISM Process

1. Presentation of Element Set

Choose two items that are to be compared and display them for the group (either on the wall or on the computer terminal). On the table in front of you, display the corresponding numbered cards side by side.

2. Discussion Leading to Paired Comparisons

Lead the group in a discussion of the items being compared. Make sure that all views are aired and that nonproductive conflict is contained.

3. Voting

Ask the group to vote on the comparison by a show of hands. A majority vote wins. Arrange your cards such that the item that people voted yes on is above the other item.

4. *Model Generation*

Repeat the process, comparing items two at a time until the group has voted on all of the items. Present the structure that has been created to the group. Ask the group, "Does this structure represent what you believe to be the sum of your decisions?"

If someone challenges the structure, do not change the structure unless the group agrees with the proposed change. Do not allow one person to unravel the work of the group.

ISM FROM THE PERSPECTIVE
OF THE READER AS FACILITATOR

The following is a step-by-step illustration of Interpretive Structural Modeling (ISM). In this example, ISM is being used to establish priorities. After you have the items you want to array in a priority order and before you meet with the group to assist them with their decision making, it is necessary to prepare the materials you will need.

1. The relationship. Although ISM allows someone to use any relationship that permits for the paired comparison of items, in setting priorities I recommend that you use the relationship:

IS AN EQUAL OR HIGHER PRIORITY THAN

2. A way to array each of the elements. You can use a variety of ways to present the items to the decision-making group. I recommend that you put each item on a sheet of paper or a placard, so that what the decision-making group sees is (a) an item, (b) the relationship, and (c) another item. The following is an example:

> ### 3. Repairing the roof of the gym

IS AN EQUAL OR HIGHER PRIORITY THAN

> ### 5. Building a new basketball court for the playground

3. A set of cards with numbers on them. The cards are needed for the facilitator to keep track of the group's decision making; 3×5 cards with large numbers written on them work just fine.

It takes a very experienced facilitator to manage alone all aspects of the priority-setting process. It will help if there are at least two facilitators. Three are even better. The tasks that the facilitator have to perform are:

1. Facilitate the group discussion of the items.
2. Keep track of the group's preferences.
3. Array the items for the group's viewing.

If there are two facilitators, one should perform tasks 1 and 3, while the other performs task 2.

Explain whatever the person who introduced you did not explain. This might include:

- Why the work they are about to do is important.

  As you know, the priorities you decide on will be used by the Board as they prepare their capital budget for the next 5 years.

- How what they are about to do fits with the organization's activities.

  This is the third stage in the capital decision-making process. First, each of the departments identified what their needs were, and then there were hearings that allowed each department head to make a case for their needs. After we are done today, it will be up to the Board to take the advice that will come from this process and prepare the capital budget.

- How the items that are about to be considered were generated. This may be included in the previous step or it could include additional detail, such as:

  The Board asked the controller to cost out each projected capital improvement. Then the decision was made to consider at least one item from each department and only items that cost more than $50,000.

- The steps in the process.

  I am about to put up two of the items you will be considering. I will then ask you to explain why you believe that one is a higher priority than the other. After you have completed your deliberation, I will call for a vote. You will continue that procedure until you have considered all of the items. When you have made all of the paired comparisons that are needed, I will show you the priority structure that you created.

- The rules of the process.

  The rules are: A majority vote decides. A tie vote counts as a "yes" vote, because *yes* also means *equal*. If it is not obvious to me from your

> discussion that you mean *higher* by your vote, I will have to switch the order of the items and ask you to vote the other way. You may want to establish that the items are equal in priority.

It is also useful to illustrate why they are utilizing what appears to be a complicated procedure to set priorities.

> Usually when we vote, using parliamentary procedure, on whether or not to fund a capital improvement, we imply a comparison with all of the other decisions we might make. But because there are hundreds of possible decisions, that is very hard to do. Who knows, for example, how many ways we can rank-order 15 items? That's right (if someone knows!), the answer is 15 factorial, which when calculated is more than 1.8 billion ways. So, if done honestly, each decision we make is much more complicated than a simple yes or no.

You should tell them at the outset, and remind them throughout the process, that:

> All of the items have a high priority or we would not be considering them, but the outcome will be useful to you only if you differentiate the relative priority of the items. That is, you need to make choices between them. But just because you are saying that one item has a higher priority, it does not mean that the other item is unimportant.

As explained above, the same procedure is repeated for each comparison:

> Show the group a pair of items.
> Ask them to give their reasons why they would prefer to vote yes or no.
> Ask them to vote.
> Record the vote.
> Start the same sequence again, until the process is complete.

The following is an example of the choices you would have to make if you wanted to conduct the process with five items. The setting for this example is a school board that is determining the relative priority of five potential capital expenditures.

1. Adding six science laboratory stations at the high school.
2. Paving the access road at West elementary.
3. Repairing the roof of the gym.
4. Building the addition to South elementary.
5. Building a new basketball court for the junior high playground.

What the school board, who will be making the decisions, sees are the items on the left. What the facilitator sees, in order to keep track of the group's decisions, are the cards on the right. It is recommended that you lay them on a table so they are viewed only by the facilitator.

The first pair of items the group will be shown are 1 and 2.

Occasionally a shorthand expression, 1 R 2, is used to refer to the comparison of two items. It means that item 1 is first, then the relationship, then 2.

The group sees:	*The facilitator sees:*
1. Adding six science stations	1 2

IS AN EQUAL OR HIGHER
PRIORITY THAN

2. Paving the access road

After the group has an opportunity to give their reasons why they prefer one or the other of the options, call for the vote. If the vote is "no" (to 1 R 2), then the group has established that they believe 2 is a higher priority than 1, and the facilitator should display the outcome for her view.

The group sees:	*The facilitator sees:*
	2
	1

If the vote is "yes" (to 1 R 2)—which means that the group believes that item 1 is an equal or higher priority than item 2—the facilitator should display the two items in reverse order and ask the group to discuss them and to vote again. The facilitator cannot assume that the original vote means that item 1 is a higher priority than item 2. The group may believe that they are of equal priority.

The group sees:	*The facilitator sees:*
2. Paving the access road	1 2

IS AN EQUAL OR HIGHER
PRIORITY THAN

1. Adding six science stations

If the vote is "no" (to 2 R 1), then the group has established that they believe 1 is a higher priority than 2 and the facilitator should display the outcome:

The group sees:	*The facilitator sees:*
	1
	2

If the group votes "yes" (to 2 R 1), which means they have voted "yes" both ways, the group has indicated that the items are of equal value and the facilitator should display the outcome:

The group sees:	*The facilitator sees:*
	1 2

Assume that they voted "no" to the original choice (1 R 2), so the outcome is:

The group sees:	*The facilitator sees:*
	2
	1

The facilitator should display the next item, 3, so that it is compared with item 1.

The group sees:	*The facilitator sees:*
3. Repairing the gym roof	2
	1 3
IS AN EQUAL OR HIGHER PRIORITY THAN	

1. Adding science stations

Note that the facilitator, for her own use, places the new item, 3, next to the item that it is being compared with, 1. If, after the discussion, the group votes "no" (to 3 R 1), which means that the group believes that 3 is not an equal or higher priority than 1, the facilitator should display the outcome:

The group sees:	The facilitator sees:
	2
	1
	3

There is no reason to compare 3 with 2 because the group already established that they believe 2 is a higher priority than 1. If the group votes "yes" (to 3 R 1), and the items are presented in reverse order (1 R 3), and the group votes "yes" again, indicating that the group believes the two items are of equal priority, the facilitator should display the outcome:

The group sees:	The facilitator sees:
	2
	1 3

If the group votes "yes" (to 3 R 1) and after the items are presented in reverse order (1 R 3) the group votes "no," indicating that the group believes that 3 is a higher priority than 1, the group then should be asked to consider the relative priority between 3 and 2.

The group sees:	The facilitator sees:
3. Repairing the gym roof	2 3
	1
IS AN EQUAL OR HIGHER PRIORITY THAN	
2. Paving the access road	

If, after discussion, the group votes "no" (to 3 R 2), indicating that they believe 2 is a higher priority than 3, the facilitator should display the outcome:

The group sees:	The facilitator sees:
	2
	3
	1

If the group votes "yes" (to 3 R 2) and the items are presented in reverse order (2 R 3) and the group votes "yes" again, indicating the group believes the two items are of equal priority, the facilitator should display the outcome:

The group sees:	*The facilitator sees:*
	2 3
	1

If the group votes "yes" (to 3 R 2) and the items are presented in reverse order (2 R 3) and the group votes "no," indicating that the group believes 3 is a higher priority than 2, then the facilitator should display the outcome:

The group sees:	*The facilitator sees:*
	3
	2
	1

Continue in this fashion. Each new item can be considered in relation to any other item. A good rule of thumb is for the facilitator to begin about the middle of the structure (that is displayed for the facilitator). So, if the facilitator has something like the following . . .

The group sees:	*The facilitator sees:*
	2
	3
	1
	4

. . . she should begin by considering 5 R 1 or 5 R 3. The vote will tell the facilitator whether to move up or down the structure. For example, if it is established that 5 is a higher priority than 1, 5 should be compared to 3. If it is established that 5 is a lower priority than 1, it should be compared to 4. If the group votes "yes" both ways, they have established that the two items are on the same level. For example, if they establish that 5 and 1 are of equal priority, the structure the facilitator sees should look like:

The group sees:	*The facilitator sees:*
	2
	3
	1 5
	4

Remember, the group only sees the two items that the facilitator displays for them.

5

When to Use the Processes

This chapter provides criteria that can be used to guide someone in the use of the three processes.

The following questions can guide your decision regarding which of the three processes should be used in order to help a group be more productive.

Which function do you need to perform? Do you want to generate, develop, or select ideas? Table 5.1 suggests which functions are met best by each of the processes.

Which of the problems that occur in interacting groups do you need to circumvent? Do you want to make certain that (1) the group produces more than a few ideas, (2) it is not dominated by one of the members, (3) there is participation by all of the members, (4) the group does not respond too strongly to the status of one of the members, (5) the group is not unduly influenced by political problems, or (6) the group does not fix on the first idea or just a few ideas? Table 5.2 suggests which of the processes would be most effective in addressing each of the problems.

Which of the processes enable you to be productive? The previous chart suggests which of the processes allow you to circumvent problems

Table 5.1
Which Function Do You Need to Perform?

	NGT	Ideawriting	ISM
Generate Ideas	√		
Develop Ideas		√	
Select Ideas			√

√ = Principal Purpose

Table 5.2

Which Problem Do You Need to Circumvent?

	NGT	Ideawriting	ISM
(1) Only a few ideas are produced	■	☐	
(2) The group is dominated by one of its members	☐	☐	
(3) All group members do not participate	■	☐	
(4) The status of one of the members has an undue influence on the group	☐	☐	
(5a) The Chair has too much authority	☐	☐	☐
(5b) The group rigidly follows rules of procedure	☐	☐	☐
(6) The group "fixes" on the first idea or on just a few ideas	■	☐	

■ = The best process to address the problem.
☐ = The process is helpful in addressing the problem.

Table 5.3

How Can You Be More Productive?

	NGT	Ideawriting	ISM
(1a) Consumes a small amount of time (so busy people can participate)	√	√	
(1b) Produces substantial results	√	√	√
(2) Enables people to work effectively in stranger groups	√	√	

√ = The process meets the criteria very well.

that inhibit the productivity of groups. Additional concerns are which processes (1) enable a substantial amount of work to be accomplished in a brief time period and (2) enable people to work effectively in groups that do not have a history of working together? See Table 5.3.

Which of the processes best meets the assumptions of second-generation design methods? Which of the processes (1) allows for argumentation of a variety of issues, (2) enables the examination of the relationship

Table 5.4
How Do the Processes Meet the Assumptions
of Second Generation Design Methods?

	NGT	Ideawriting	ISM
(1) Allows argumentation of issues			√
(2) Enable examination of the relationship between issues			√
(3) Can clarify ideas	√	√	√
(4) Allows client to maintain control	√	√	√
(5) Can be used without a clear-cut image of the solution	√	√	√

√ = The process meets the criteria very well.

Table 5.5
Which Processes are Easiest to Use?

	NGT	Ideawriting	ISM
(1) Facilitation	4	2	5
(2a) Support: equipment/materials	2	2	3
(2b) Support: technology	1	1	5*
(2c) Support: knowledge of process	2	2	4
(3) Effort required to teach prospective users	3	2	5

*If a computer is used; a "1" if a computer is not used.

1 = none   2 = little   3 = some   4 = substantial   5 = very substantial

among issues, (3) can clarify ideas, (4) allows the client (the individual or group with the problem) to maintain control over the process, and (5) can be used even though there is not a clear-cut image of the solution? Table 5.4 suggests which of the processes best meets these assumptions.

Which of the processes is the easiest to use? Which of the three (1) requires the least amount of facilitation, (2) requires the least support (equipment/materials, technology, knowledge of process), and (3) is the easiest to teach to prospective users? Table 5.5 rates each of the processes in terms of ease of use.

6

Beyond Process

This chapter describes principles that are not dependent on the use of any particular process and can be used to enhance group productivity.

The purpose of this book is to provide clear, complete, useful descriptions of three task-oriented processes that can be used to help groups be more productive: to help them generate, develop, and select ideas. The previous chapters have made a number of claims about the benefits of using the processes, especially that using them enables the participation of a wide range of people and can help circumvent problems that occur in interacting groups.

In order to achieve the book's purpose, it has been necessary to provide didactic descriptions that emphasize the stages of the processes. Such an emphasis can be misleading, because it gives the false impression that each of the processes is an end in itself.

The purposes of this chapter are to clear up potential misconceptions and to identify principles that group facilitators can use to assist groups. The goal is to identify principles that are beyond process, that are illustrated by but are independent of any particular method or technique.

The processes presented in this book are not ends in themselves. The processes are seldom used independently. It is usually necessary to link them together and with other processes (such as traditional interacting meetings) to enhance group productivity. Linking the processes seems to produce a power that is greater than when each of them is implemented separately. One reason for the powerful result from linking processes is that it contributes to group learning about the meaning of items. Linking processes allows the group members to look at the same thing from different perspectives. If the processes are used over time, they allow a group to acquire a gestalt of its issue.

One of the processes can be used to achieve a single purpose in a broader decision-making context. For example, a strategic planning group can use a variety of means (other than those presented in this book) to identify potential strategies, then use Ideawriting to generate and develop ideas for each strategy, and then meet for a series of follow-up meetings to discuss the options that emerged. A process might be utilized to help groups do their work and to realize secondary benefits, as well. One important secondary benefit would be for the group to become more self-confident, to believe that they are capable of producing useful products. Groups occasionally flounder for a considerable period of time over their inability to accomplish assigned tasks. It is difficult for them to get started. A successful idea-generating session using NGT (or one of the other processes) might help them perform one of their tasks and thereby give them self-confidence that they can work together successfully in order to achieve their goals. Once they have gained confidence in one another and in their ability to do work together, members are likely to be a more productive group in the future.

Another, related secondary benefit is that they can help to create group spirit, a commitment to the task and to one another. People want to get along, to work smoothly together, but they do not know how. Their own behaviors often get in the way. These processes capitalize on motivation to work together.

Principle 1: *Groups will be more effective if the individual participants have an opportunity to think, and perhaps even write, before they are asked to contribute to the work of the group.*

Although groups are usually more effective than individuals in generating ideas, individuals are often more effective than groups when it comes to developing ideas. That is because research, analysis, and careful crafting of language—the skills most necessary when developing ideas—are performed better by individuals. A process like Ideawriting is uniquely useful (compared with other group processes) as a way to develop ideas, because it draws on the strengths of individual activity. Ideawriting allows the participants to write, and even to carry on a written exchange of ideas, before they begin their oral conversation. Nominal Group Technique reflects this principle when it asks the group members to silently generate ideas in writing before contributing them to the work of the group.

A group facilitator does not have to use any of the three processes presented in this book in order to benefit from this knowledge about the differences between group and individual activity. If you are about to ask a group to brainstorm ideas or even to discuss an idea, give them a few silent moments to think about the question or topic before beginning to talk.

Principle 2: *Groups are likely to be more willing to select ideas if they are not forced into a win-lose, zero-sum position. Time and circumstances permitting, they prefer the opportunity to be reflective.*

Members of a group often resist selecting among ideas. Some resist because they are motivated by the desire to keep everything equal; they operate on the assumption that to give priority to one idea is to preclude other ideas. The traditional means used to select ideas—particularly voting—reinforce this concern. Voting encourages winning and losing; it permits a zero-sum outcome (in which my gain is your loss). Interpretive Structural Modeling (ISM) is perceived by group members as a useful way to select ideas because the paired decision making is a reasonable way to make choices and because the outcome is not absolute. Even though votes are taken, they are not single, final votes.

Groups often like to take straw votes to see where they stand, because such an action seems to be a less permanent decision. Instead of voting, it is possible to have groups rate items. Even ranking is often preferable to voting, because the group members are reflecting a range of choices. Sometimes it is necessary to vote and to abide by the outcome of the vote. Try to keep those times to a minimum.

Another principle that flows directly from experience with ISM is:

Principle 3: *Decision making in groups benefits from focus.*

Often groups are asked the wrong question if they are asked, "How important is choice A?" Choice A in relation to what? All other potential choices? ISM demonstrates that it is much more effective to present groups with two choices at a time, so the question becomes, "Is choice A better than or equal to choice B?" In Nominal Group Technique, one of the reasons for having a group revote is to eliminate the items that did not get any consideration in the first vote. That enables them to focus on a delimited group of choices.

Group facilitators can act on this simple principle of focus by giving careful consideration to how choices are presented to groups. Even if an ISM is not used, it may be appropriate to ask the group to select between paired comparisons. One way to move a group toward closure is to get members' permission to remove from consideration items that do not have much importance. But they do not benefit if the focus is premature.

Principle 4: *The productivity of a group can be enhanced if the group leader collects all ideas before allowing the group to assess any of them.*

There is a tendency in groups to spend most of the time talking about the first option that is mentioned. That is because people are quick to assess the worth of ideas. A common, and unfortunately limiting, expression in society right now is "Don't just talk about it, do something." When this sense of urgency is combined with a tendency to encourage people to be glib—to speak up quickly and cleverly—the result can be poor decisions. NGT, therefore, collects all ideas before discussing them. Even if you are not using NGT, you can tell the group that you want them to suggest all possible options, that you will record the options, and that the group will not discuss any of them until all of them have been mentioned.

Principle 5: *The productivity of a group can be enhanced if a group memory is utilized.*

Part of the effectiveness of Nominal Group Technique (and, to a lesser extent, Ideawriting) is because of the group memory. A group memory is when you record the work of the group on large sheets of paper and keep that work before the group at all times. The notion of keeping a group memory is useful even if NGT or Ideawriting is not utilized.

I had an occasion to mediate the differences between some "concerned citizens" and representatives of an Indian tribe. In order to encourage them to feel as if their concerns were being heard, each of the points they made was recorded on newsprint and the sheets of newsprint were taped to the wall. This experience reinforced my belief that it is valuable to keep a group memory in almost any type of meeting. Compared to my experience in other, similar settings, both groups felt less need to keep repeating their positions (and, if they did, I could remind them that the position had been recorded) and did appear to pay more attention to the position of the other side. Groups are more likely to relax and have confidence in their leader/facilitator if they believe that their ideas have been captured. Moreover, group memories can be used to keep the group focused on the tasks and even to deal with disruptive group members (Doyle & Straus, 1976).

Principle 6: *The productivity of a group can be enhanced if the group leader encourages the members of the group to build on ("hitchhike") each other's ideas.*

Most groups, unfortunately, do not realize their full decision-making potential. In fact, one of the principal reasons for the development and use of the three processes presented in this book is to circumvent the problems that characterize most groups, to allow them to be more productive. Two of the processes—NGT and Ideawriting—purposefully capitalize on the benefits to be gained from group members building on the work of other group members. Participants in NGT are encouraged to hitchhike on the ideas that are contributed. One of the essential steps in Ideawriting is to react to and expand on the ideas expressed by others.

None of the processes has to be directly utilized in order for the group to benefit from this principle. As a facilitator, you can encourage the group members to build on one another's ideas and thereby realize one of the principal benefits of serving in a group, rather than working as individuals.

Principle 7: *Groups are more likely to be satisfied with their work if they have a sense of ownership of that work.*

Groups will take more satisfaction in their work and are more likely to abide by their own decisions if they believe that they are responsible for the final product. Groups need to feel ownership of their work. One thing that can diminish a sense of group ownership is that the group comes to believe that it is not responsible for the product that was produced. For example, if the person facilitating the NGT session writes down what he or she thinks items mean, rather than what was specifically said, the group can easily disassociate themselves from the final list. In addition, if the contributions of an individual or a group of individuals are repeatedly ignored, they will not want to claim the final product, no matter how good it appears to be. The facilitator in an ISM should interact with the group, but should never substitute his or her ideas for theirs.

A group facilitator must be careful to act as a process leader—rather than as a substantive expert—or the group is not likely to claim ownership of the product that is produced. Whether or not the processes described in this book are utilized, a group leader should keep in mind and be sensitive to the need for the group to produce its own product.

Principle 8: *Satisfaction with group participation is enhanced if the group has a sense of closure.*

In that the three processes are well-defined processes, they all have beginnings, steps or stages, and ways to end. NGT produces a list of items and indicates the preferences of the group regarding the items.

Ideawriting often has each of the groups report on the product that it produced. ISM produces a structure of ideas.

Even if one of the processes from this book is not utilized, it is beneficial to bring closure to the work of a group. The group leader should develop specific strategies that will give the group a sense that they have completed their work. A satisfying way to bring closure to a group is by developing concrete action plans for one or more of the key items. The step-by-step illustration of Ideawriting at the end of Chapter 3 presents a way to develop action plans.

Principle 9: *No process is any better than the people who participate.*

Chapter 2 explained that Nominal Group Technique is seductive, for both the participants and the group facilitator. It is easy for someone to come to believe that NGT, as well as the other processes presented in this book, can accomplish more than is possible. The processes obviously do not possess any wisdom in and of themselves. The products that are produced can be no better than the people who participate in the process. Planning for the use of any of the processes must be qualified by the realization that one cannot accomplish more in a group than what the particular members of the group are able to contribute.

SUMMARY

The three processes described in this book are not ends in themselves. They are seldom used independently, they may be used in concert with other group processes, and they may even be used to realize secondary, indirect benefits.

There are certain principles a facilitator should learn about using groups as a result of studying these three processes.

- Groups will be more effective if the individual participants have an opportunity to think, and perhaps even write, before they are asked to contribute to the work of the group.
- Groups are likely to be more willing to select ideas if they are not forced into a win-lose, zero-sum position. Time and circumstances permitting, most group members prefer the opportunity to be reflective.
- Decision making in groups benefits from focus.

- The productivity of a group can be enhanced if the group leader collects all ideas before allowing the group to assess any of them.
- The productivity of a group can be enhanced if a group memory is utilized.
- The productivity of a group can be enhanced if the group leader encourages the members of the group to build on (hitchhike) one another's ideas.
- Group members are more likely to be satisfied with their work if they have a sense of ownership of that work. Maybe the converse is more important. The person facilitating the work of the group must be careful not to jeopardize the sense that the group—not the leader or facilitator—was responsible for producing the final product.
- Satisfaction with group participation is enhanced if the group has a sense of closure.
- No process is any better than the people who participate in it.

References

Delbecq, A. L., Van de Ven, A. H., & Gustafson, D. H. (1975). *Group techniques for program planning: A guide to Nominal Group and Delphi processes.* Glenview, IL: Scott, Foresman.

Doyle, M., & Straus, D. (1976). *How to make meetings work.* New York: Jove.

Helmer, O. (1981, May). Interview. *Omni,* pp. 81-90.

Lindblom, C. D., & Cohen, D. K. (1979). *Usable knowledge: Social science and social problem-solving.* New Haven, CT: Yale University Press.

Moore, C. M. (1991). Community is where community happens. *National Civic Review, 80*(4), 352-357.

Olsen, S. A. (Ed.). (1982). *Group planning and problem-solving methods in engineering management.* New York: John Wiley.

Strauch, R. E. (1974). *A critical assessment of quantitative methodology as a policy analysis tool.* Santa Monica, CA: Rand.

Thissen, W. A. H., Sage, A. P., & Warfield, J. N. (1980). *A users' guide to public systems methodology.* Charlottesville, VA: School of Engineering and Applied Science.

Warfield, J. N. (1976). *Societal systems: Planning, policy, and complexity.* New York: John Wiley.

Warfield, J. N. (1982). *Consensus methodologies.* Charlottesville, VA: Center for Interactive Management.

Weiss, C. H. (Ed.). (1977). *Using social research in public policy making.* Lexington, MA: Lexington.

Williams, H. (1980). Some thoughts on pursuing goals in the three-county area. In C. M. Moore, H. Williams, & S. Shapiro (Eds.), *What issues, problems, and opportunities should be addressed in order to make the three-county region of Adair, Cherokee, and Sequoyah a better place to live in the 1980s?* Dayton, OH: Kettering Foundation.

About the Author

Carl M. Moore recently retired from Kent State University where he served as Professor in Communication Studies for 26 years. A former Fellow of the Academy for Contemporary Problems and the National Training and Development Service, he is a senior associate in community problem solving with the Urban Center of the College of Urban Affairs at Cleveland State University.

Dr. Moore served as cochair of the Governor's Commission on Peace and Conflict Management that proposed legislation to create Ohio's statewide Office of Dispute Resolution and Conflict Management. He was responsible (along with James C. Coke) for the development of the Negotiated Investment Strategy (NIS) model and evaluated the first applications of the NIS in St. Paul, Minnesota; Columbus, Ohio; Gary, Indiana; and for the state of Connecticut. On two occasions he mediated the state of Mississippi's allocation of the Social Service Bloc Grant monies. He also has mediated the Bridgeport (Connecticut) Initiative, a plan for the development of land use and annexation policies in Arapahoe County (Colorado), and community-wide decision making in Clark County (Ohio) regarding the Community Action Agency. He has been responsible for negotiating faculty contracts at Kent State University and for facilitating/mediating disputes involving the Cherokee Nation, Winnebago Indians, Connecticut Social Service Tri-Partite Commission, various public service agencies, foundations, and local and state governments. He was program chair for the 1991 National Conference on Peacemaking and Conflict Resolution (theme: "Community in Conflict") and serves on the board of NCPCR.

Much of Dr. Moore's time is spent facilitating the planning and decision making of a wide range of governments and not-for-profit agencies. His clients range from White House conferences to communitywide agencies to local school districts.

Dr. Moore has assisted community leadership programs throughout the United States. He has worked with the Lilly Endowment on their program in community leadership and with the board of the National Association of Community Leadership Organizations (NACLO), writes the "Consultant Corner" column for *Leadership News*, and has planned and presented programs at many NACLO national conferences.

He has served as an academic specialist in Singapore for the United States Information Agency and in Czechoslovakia for the program in community development of the Institute for East-West Security Studies. He has taught courses in leadership and negotiation for the master's degree in public policy (focus on Southeast Asia) offered by the National University of Singapore in conjunction with the Harvard Institute on International Development and has conducted a workshop on facilitative leadership for senior officers and middle managers in the government of Brunei and for senior civil service ministers from the six ASEAN countries (Brunei, Indonesia, Malaysia, Philippines, Singapore, Thailand).

His publications include *Group Techniques for Idea Building, A Colorful Quilt: The Community Leadership Story, The Facilitator's Manual,* and articles in *Nation's Cities Weekly, Journal of Intergroup Relations, Communications Strategies in the Practice of Lawyering, Public Administration Review,* and the *National Civic Review.*